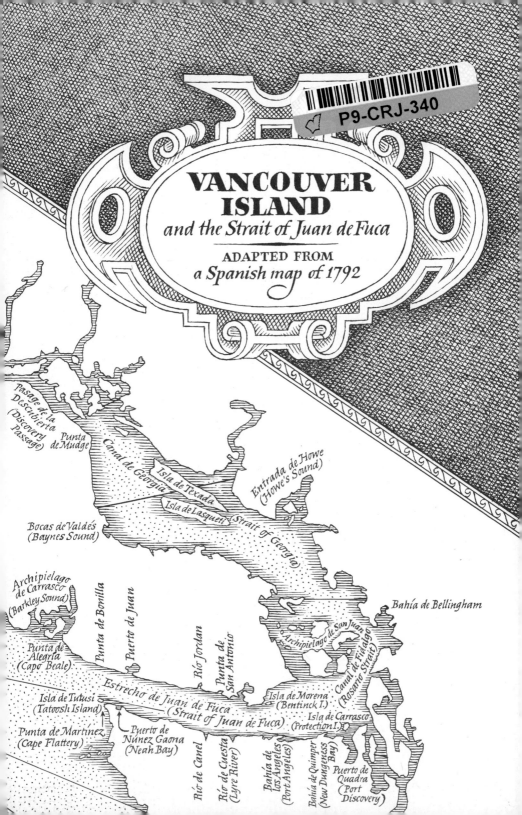

# VANCOUVER ISLAND
## and the Strait of Juan de Fuca

ADAPTED FROM
*a Spanish map of 1792*

Pasage de la Descubierta
(Discovery Passage)

Punta de Mudge

Canal de Georgia

Isla de Texada

Isla de Lasquetí

Entrada de Howe
(Howe's Sound)

Strait of Georgia

Bocas de Valdés
(Baynes Sound)

Archipielago de Carrasco
(Barkley Sound)

Punta de Bonilla

Puerto de Juan

Río Jordan

Punta de San Antonio

Bahía de Bellingham

Archipielago de San Juan

Canal de Fidalgo
(Rosario Strait)

Punta de Alegría
(Cape Beale)

Isla de Tutusi
(Tatoosh Island)

Estrecho de Juan de Fuca
(Strait of Juan de Fuca)

Isla de Morena
(Bentinck I.)

Isla de Carrasco
(Protection I.)

Punta de Martínez
(Cape Flattery)

Puerto de Núnez Gaona
(Neah Bay)

Río de Canel

Río de Cuesta
(Lyre River)

Bahía de los Angeles
(Port Angeles)

Bahía de Quimper
(New Dungeness Bay)

Puerto de Quadra
(Port Discovery)

MONOGRAPH 50
THE AMERICAN ETHNOLOGICAL SOCIETY
ROBERT F. SPENCER, EDITOR

# NOTICIAS DE NUTKA

An Account of Nootka Sound in 1792

---

BY JOSÉ MARIANO MOZIÑO

*Translated and edited by Iris Higbie Wilson*

*Foreword by Philip Drucker*

---

UNIVERSITY OF WASHINGTON PRESS

SEATTLE AND LONDON

*TO PAUL*

# FOREWORD

I N THE closing decades of the eighteenth century and the beginning ones of the nineteenth the Northwest Coast of America, a wilderness of jagged mountains slashed by a network of
narrow sheer-walled fiords and inhabited by warlike Indian
groups, was a focus of attention in the capitals of Western civilization well around on the far side of the globe. Remote, acces-
sible only by perilous routes skirting the Antarctic or crossing
Siberia's frozen wastelands, the region nonetheless figured in the
political schemes of empire builders and in plans of proponents
of the get-rich-quick school of finance who hoped to exploit its
bonanza of peltries. Sailing the coast's myriad channels, sometimes on an "ash breeze"—towed by a whaleboat under oars—
where the channel was too narrow for a sailing ship to beat up-
wind, scouting for sheltered anchorages with good holding
ground, searching for the Indians' encampments, always with an
eye out for the mythical Northwest Passage that would reduce
sailing time from North Atlantic to North Pacific, were a throng
of the hardiest sailors of the shores of the Atlantic. Naval officers
from England, Spain, Russia, and an ill-starred one from France,
mindful of the rights conferred by "discovery," explored the
coast. Hard-bitten "gentlemen-adventurers," more adventurous
than gentlemanly, competing for fortunes in sea-otter furs, sometimes preceded the naval people into concealed bays and har-

bors. The heavy-handed Baranof, a man of commerce despite his quasi-official status, with his horde of peonized Aleut hunters; a host of British merchant-skippers; and another host of Americans, mostly with Boston as their home port, combed the coast for lustrous pelts.

In inevitable constant confrontation with the swashbucklers from the Atlantic were the Indians of the Northwest Coast. They were numerous. They were bold: early in the series of contacts they had learned that the pale-skinned bearded strangers were not supernatural beings but men who could bleed and die. And the Indians had to be dealt with, for they were the sea-hunters from whom the precious sea-otter hides were obtained. The journals of the early voyagers, officials and traders alike, Cook and Vancouver, Malaspina and La Pérouse, Meares, Dixon and Portlock, Kendrick and Gray, contain a wealth of data on the Indians, direct observations on appearance, dress, inevitably on weaponry, on canoes and houses, on memorials and "totem poles." These bits of information on the native cultures at the dawn of the historic period are of great significance to students of human culture not only as aids in defining the precontact cultures of the area but also as primary data for studies of culture change, as materials to be compared with those of the more recent ethnographic reports.

One outstanding deficiency of these invaluable data is that they are limited in content to such materials as could be observed directly: whether arrows were tipped with metal or bone points, styles in dress and ornament, forms of houses and canoes, and the like. Aspects of nonmaterial culture—social structure and behavior, religious belief—are not touched on. Not only was time short, but communication was minimal. Information on these topics cannot be requested by, nor reported by, gestures.

There is one exception referable to the early period: Don Joseph Mariano Moziño's description of the natives of Nootka Sound, by coincidence the same Indians described in detailed fashion a number of years later by their sometime captive, John R. Jewitt. The circumstances that brought Moziño to Nootka are related in the present work and need not be repeated here. What is important to note is, first, that Moziño was a scientist by training and, second, that he attempted to assemble data for and to present an ethnographic description of the sort that a modern ethnologist might prepare. If on comparison with modern studies his work has certain deficiencies, it is nonetheless the fullest and best account of any Northwest Coast group before Jewitt's florid (ghostwritten?) "Narrative," and in point of fact contains much material not mentioned by the captive. (Jewitt's journal, brief and understandably morbid, gives little ethnographic detail, though it contains much between-the-lines information on economic patterns. The slave Jewitt was often hungry.)

Moziño was, of course, carrying on a tradition of Spanish colonialism that dated back to at least the mid-sixteenth century, when data on Indian languages and customs were collected systematically. His predecessors in linguistic and ethnologic studies included such figures as the Bishop Diego de Landa and Fray Bernardino de Sahagún. While the clergy had a special interest in this work, Spanish secular administrators also found utility in some topics; the neat adaptation of the Aztec tribute system to make it a source of colonial revenues demonstrates the point.

That this work, a late-eighteenth-century ethnography, an account of a living functioning primitive culture, should be so little known by historians and anthropologists is due to several factors. First are the vicissitudes of the original manuscript report, submitted apparently in the proper and official number of laboriously handwritten copies, only to be buried in the archives. Bureaucracy was ever thus. This history is reported by Dr. Wilson in her commentary; I shall not enlarge on it. But when eventually an admirer of Moziño found the manuscript a century or so later, and arranged to publish it in Mexico, the publication was in a skimpy edition of few copies. To make matters worse, the published version appeared in 1913, presumably in one of the rare and brief interludes of tranquillity in the seventeen-year-long Mexican revolution. Distribution was less than good. Not many libraries in this country own copies.

I, if I may be permitted to personalize this Foreword a bit, acquired my copy of the 1913 edition of Moziño thirty-some years ago on my return from my first visit to the Nootka. The late W. A. ("Billy") Newcombe gave it to me. He had acquired it somehow but could not read it, and he knew that I knew a bit of Spanish. That was another factor limiting use of the account. Northwest Coast historians of the older generation, except for Wagner, did not control Spanish; the same seems to have been true of older generation anthropologists. Consequently, what few copies were available of this rich source gathered dust, their pages unturned.

For this reason Dr. Wilson's clear and precise translation of Moziño's report on the Nootka (it should be noted that the original contains some literary archaisms that only thorough understanding of the Spanish language, not dictionaries, can resolve) is of importance. This would be true had she presented only the bare ethnologic description. But she has given Moziño's report historical perspective by including its background in terms of the situation of Spanish imperialism of the time, anthropological perspective through annotations and comparisons with later ethnological materials, and biological precision by a careful check of Moziño's faunal and floral identifications. The total result is a signal contribution to Northwest Coast history and ethnology.

PHILIP DRUCKER

# PREFACE

NOTICIAS DE NUTKA was written in Spanish by botanist-naturalist José Mariano Moziño following his visit to Nootka Sound, Vancouver Island, from April 29 to September 21, 1792, as a member of the expedition of Juan Francisco de la Bodega y Quadra. Extending beyond the scope of a scientific report, Moziño's comprehensive account is a unique ethnographic and historical study of the Northwest Coast. A Nootkan-Spanish dictionary, drawings by artist Atanasio Echeverría, and a catalogue of plants and animals classified according to the Linnaean system supplement the work. Although there are several manuscript copies of the "Noticias," I have translated herein the one published in Mexico by the Sociedad Mexicana de Geografía y Estadística in 1913. It is a faithful transcription of a manuscript which its editor, historian Alberto M. Carreño, thought was possibly Moziño's original narrative written in the author's own hand. The results of my own study indicate that it was an early version, probably not the first, copied by a scribe.

The manuscript edited by Carreño consisted of two parts: "Noticias de Nutka" and an accompanying dictionary, both undated, and a description of the Mexican volcano of Tuxtla. The last item was dated and signed at San Andrés de Tuxtla on November 27, 1793, the day on which Moziño completed his investigation of the volcano's eruption. I believe the material concerning Nootka to have been completed earlier and perhaps recopied at Tuxtla, since Moziño had returned to Mexico on February 2, 1793. A letter from Martín Sessé, director of the Royal Scientific Expedition to New Spain, to Viceroy Revilla Gigedo, dated May 9, 1793, referred to Moziño's "Noticias" as having been left in Mexico City before April 20. No date except the year 1793 appears on the title page. When compared with other versions, the manuscript published in Mexico shows some variation; nevertheless the overall content is essentially the same in all. I have called attention in my notes to significant changes, additions, or omissions among the various copies with which I have worked.

In his Introduction to *Noticias de Nutka*, Carreño described Moziño as "one of the most conspicuous scientific personalities that New Spain produced in the eighteenth century." He explained that Mexico delayed publication of this important account because no copy of the manuscript could be located until 1880, when one was discovered in the Sociedad Mexicana's own library in Mexico City. The 1913 edition did not include the drawings because they were not in the local archives. Since then two sets of illustrations and several additional copies of Moziño's account have been located. I have compared Carreño's published version with four other manuscripts. One is found in the Revilla Gigedo Papers belonging to the private collection of Irving W. Robbins of Atherton, California; two are located in the archives of the Museo Naval, Ministerio de Marina (Madrid); and the fourth is in the Frederick W. Beinecke Collection of the Yale University Library, New Haven, Connecticut. Other copies of "Noticias de Nutka" are found in the Biblioteca del Palacio Nacional (Madrid) and in the Angrand Collection in the Bibliothèque Nationale (Paris). It was published for the first time in several parts in Volumes VII and VIII (1803 and 1804) of the *Gazeta de Guatemala*.

The Yale manuscript varies most frequently from the Carreño

[ xii ]

edition and bears the title "Relación de la Isla de Mazarredo" ("Account of the Island of Mazarredo") in place of "Noticias de Nutka." This version gives repeated evidence of having been composed from Moziño's work by some literate person who was acquainted with the events described or whose presence at Nootka was coincident with the composition of the "Noticias." Frequent changes, especially the substitution of the third person plural or such phrases as "the members of the expedition," "the Spaniards," or "our Botanists" for the first person singular, make it apparent that this was not Moziño's own narrative. From the handwriting and other internal evidence, it could well have been the work of Josef Cardero, scribe of the Alcalá Galiano-Valdés expedition of 1792 who was later assigned to the Naval Department at Cádiz. A number of footnotes were added in this copy, as indicated below.

Bodega y Quadra's official journal, found both in the archives of the Ministerio de Asuntos Exteriores (Madrid) and in the Revilla Gigedo Papers belonging to Irving W. Robbins, includes the drawings and maps which illustrate "Noticias de Nutka," the catalogue of plants and animals, and a copy of the dictionary. Entitled "Viaje a la Costa N.O. de la America Septentrional . . . en el año de 1792" ("Voyage to the Northwest Coast of North America . . . in the year 1792"), Bodega y Quadra's narrative describes the expedition's stay at Nootka and California (October 10, 1792, to January 14, 1793) and gives much supporting evidence to Moziño's findings.

The several copies of Moziño's dictionary vary in organization, selection of words, phonetic spelling, and other minor details. I have translated the one contained in the archives of the Ministerio de Asuntos Exteriores because it appears to be the most accurate in comparison with all the others. Also, except for verbs, it is organized by subject matter instead of alphabetically in Spanish. The dictionary published in Carreño's *Noticias* is incomplete and in a number of places incorrect, probably as the result of faulty copying. Carreño supplemented the dictionary with additional words taken from a copy found with the Alcalá Galiano-Valdés journal, but there are still some deletions. Variant spellings of Nootkan words have been included if they differed significantly.

Most of Moziño's unpublished papers are housed in the archives of the Real Jardín Botánico, Museo Nacional de Ciencias Naturales, and Real Academia Nacional de Medicina in Madrid. They consist of correspondence both to and from Moziño, several essays by him on aspects of botany and medicine, hundreds of scientific descriptions of plants of New Spain and Guatemala, and even some poems in Latin. Other documents involving Moziño and his work are located in the Archivo General de la Nación in Mexico, Archivo General de Indias in Sevilla, Archivo Histórico Nacional and Museo Naval in Madrid, and the British Museum in London. Some botanical plates from the Nootka area exist in the library of the Conservatoire Botanique in Geneva, Switzerland, and are described in Alphonse de Candolle's *Calques des dessins de la Flore de Mexique de Mociño et Sessé* (Geneva, 1874). I first became acquainted with these materials in 1960–61 as a fellow of the Del Amo Foundation (Los Angeles and Madrid) and translated many of them in the preparation of my doctoral dissertation. A grant from the American Philosophical Society in 1964–65 made it possible for me to review them in greater detail.

In addition to *Noticias de Nutka*, Moziño's published works include several articles on medical, botanical, and philosophical subjects. He coauthored, with Martín Sessé, *Flora Mexicana* and *Plantae Novae Hispaniae*, published by the Sociedad Mexicana de Historia Natural in 1885 and 1889, respectively. These volumes gave Moziño and his mentor Sessé long-overdue recognition for their pioneer work in collecting and classifying thousands of Mexican plants.

The translation of eighteenth-century Spanish documents is not easy. Sentences at times seem interminable, while shifting among tenses and persons, and often a single sentence makes up an entire paragraph. Although ambiguous in some parts, "Noticias de Nutka" is generally clear and shows Moziño to be a keen observer capable of accurate and lively description. Without sacrificing the original flavor of the Spanish, I have attempted to convey the precise meaning of the author by means of modern rules of punctuation and capitalization. I have standardized the spelling of proper names either by substituting their common English equivalents—for example, Vancouver for Wancower, Fitz-Herbert for Tit-her-vert, Wickinanish for Huiquinanis, Maquinna for Macuina—or by adopting the most frequently employed spelling of Nootkan words or names. *Catlati* (brothers of the chief), for example, also appears as *Kac-la-tis* or *Katlate;* Chief Tlu-pana-nutl is also Hua-pa-na-nutl; Princess Izto-coti-clemot is variously Hui-cocoti-tlemos, Istocoti-Tlemoc, or Yzto-coti-clemos. Wherever possible, present-day names are given for geographical locations.

The task of translating and editing this work was made considerably lighter by the constant encouragement and advice of Professor Donald C. Cutter. It would be difficult to overestimate the benefit of his guidance and companionship in the archives of Mexico and Spain during the years of our "mutual research" into the history of Spanish exploration along the Pacific Coast. His careful reading of the manuscript has been invaluable.

Captain Roberto Barreiro-Meiro of the Museo Naval in Madrid gave cheerful aid in the tedious job of comparing copies of the "Noticias," and Luis Antonio Gallego helped in translation and research. Special thanks are due Federico Isidro Sánchez for patient assistance in finding the exact meaning of difficult Spanish passages, Mrs. Cynthia van Stralen for compiling the bibliography, and Miss Julie Becklund for typing the manuscript. Professors Philip Drucker, University of Kentucky, and Wilson Duff, University of British Columbia, provided excellent suggestions for anthropological notes; and Irving W. Robbins generously allowed me to use his collection of the Revilla Gigedo papers. I owe a particular debt of gratitude to Professor Gordon A. Clopine, San Bernardino Valley College, for his long hours of work in supplying common names for the flora and much of the fauna in Appendix B. I also wish to thank Professor Curt W. Spanis, University of San Diego, and staff members of the Los Angeles County Museum and San Diego Museum of Natural History for their help in this regard.

Others who have given valuable guidance, and whose encouragement and interest have contributed to the completion of this work, include: Admiral Julio Guillén y Tato, director, and Father Vicente Vela, assistant director, of the Museo Naval (Madrid); Professor W. Michael Mathes, University of San Francisco; Professor Andrew F. Rolle, Occidental College (Los Angeles); J. Ignacio Rubio Mañe, director of the Archivo General de la Nación (Mexico); Willard Ireland, director of the Provincial Archives of British Columbia (Victoria, B.C.); Miss María de los Angeles Calatayud, Museo Nacional de Ciencias Naturales, and Miss Irene Carrascosa, Real Jardín Botánico (Madrid); the staff members of the Conservatoire Botanique (Geneva), Yale University Library, and of the other research institutions which I visited. Mrs. Charlotte Cutter, Miss Gloria Gomez, Miss Carolee Ann Meachum, and Mr. Craig S. Engstrand also deserve thanks for many special favors connected with this work.

IRIS HIGBIE WILSON

San Diego, California
April 27, 1970

# CONTENTS

Contents

# Contents

# iLLustratiOns

Plates 1 and 2 are reproduced by courtesy of the Sociedad Mexicana de Geografía y Estadística, Mexico, D.F. Plates 3 through 24 are reproduced by courtesy of the Ministerio de Asuntos Exteriores, Madrid. The endpaper map is adapted from a map in "Planos geográficos y dibujos para ilustrar el Diario de D. Juan Francisco de la Bodega y Quadra," Revilla Gigedo Papers, Vol. XXIX, Private Collection of Irving W. Robbins, Atherton, California.

FOLLOWING PAGE XXXII

1. *Title page of "Noticias de Nutka"*
2. *First page of Article No. 1*
3. *Map of the anchorage of Nootka*
4. *Map of the interior channels of the Port of Nootka*
5. *A Nootka* tais, *or chief*
6. *The wife of a Nootka chief*
7. *Nootka noblewoman with a child in the cradle*
8. *A Nootka commoner*

FOLLOWING PAGE 10

9. *"Sardine" fishing*
10. *Interior view of Maquinna's house*

[ xxi ]

## Illustrations

# INTRODUCTION

Noticias de nutka is a contemporary account of Nootka Sound, Vancouver Island, and of its natives during the last quarter of the eighteenth century. The author, José Mariano Moziño Suárez de Figueroa,[1] was the official botanist appointed by the viceroy of New Spain to accompany the expedition of Juan Francisco de la Bodega y Quadra to Nootka Sound in 1792, a voyage frequently referred to as the Expedition of the Limits to the North of California.[2] The *Noticias* was not, however, the usual botanical report. Moziño's work was a thorough and comprehensive study that was scheduled for publication in the Uni-

[1] Moziño's name according to his certificate of baptism at Temascaltepec, Mexico (September 24, 1775), was Joseph Mariano Mosiño Losada, his parents being Don Juan Antonio Mosiño and Doña Manuela Losada. The three common spellings of his name are Moziño, Mociño, and Mosiño; I have adopted the first, which was most frequently used by Moziño himself. Such variations in spelling were characteristic of the time. "Suárez de Figueroa" was most likely an additional family name.

[2] "La Expedición de Limites al Norte de California." Bodega y Quadra's official journal bears the title "Viaje a la Costa N. O. de la América Septentrional por Don Juan Francisco de la Bodega Y Quadra, del Orden de Santiago, Capitán de Navío de la Real Armada, y Comandante del Departamento de San Blas en las Fragatas de su mando *Sta. Gertrudis, Aránzazu, Princesa* y Goleta *Activo* en el año de 1792," MS 145, Archivo del Ministerio de Asuntos Exteriores (Madrid) and Revilla Gigedo Papers, Vol. XXIX, Private Collection of Irving W. Robbins, Atherton, Calif.; hereafter cited as Bodega y Quadra, "Viaje de 1792."

versal History of North America.[3] Alone, the account represented a segment of little-known Spanish scientific interest in the lands and peoples that lay within the New World dominion claimed by Spain. More generally, *Noticias de Nutka* epitomized that nation's participation in the intellectual enlightenment of the eighteenth century.

As the full title of his work suggests, Moziño discusses almost every aspect of Nootka and its Indians at the time of their initial contact with European civilization. His experience in the Pacific Northwest not only gave the Spanish scientist rare insight into the reaction of these Indians to foreign visitors, but it allowed him to describe their daily life with unique detail. Moziño wrote:

> Our residence of more than four months on that island enabled me to learn about the various customs of the natives, their religion, and their system of government. I believe that I am the first person who has been able to gather such information, and this was because I learned their language sufficiently to converse with them.[4]

If Spain's plans for a universal history had materialized, the *Noticias* would have served to acquaint Europeans with a strategic area of the Pacific Northwest and provided natural scientists with an abundance of untapped source material.

The projects of Carlos III, the reigning Spanish monarch from 1759 to 1788, were many and varied. At home, this clever and ambitious member of the Bourbon family centralized the administration of government, increased revenues, constructed

[3] Donald C. Cutter, "Spanish Scientific Exploration along the Pacific Coast," in *The American West—An Appraisal*, edited by Robert G. Ferris (Santa Fe: Museum of New Mexico Press, 1963), p. 155.

[4] See p. 9. Others had gained some data previously, but Moziño was in a better position to observe this type of activity. It is unlikely, however, that he became completely fluent in the language in such a short time; he must have been forced to rely at times upon the Indians' (and especially Chief Maquinna's) moderate knowledge of Spanish. Wherever possible, I have compared his observations with studies made by contemporary visitors to Nootka Sound and by modern ethnographers.

roads and canals, improved agriculture, reorganized the military, fostered both immigration to the Peninsula and emigration to the Americas, and, in general, gained a new prestige for Spain among European nations. The king continued his program in the Indies and instituted significant governmental and economic reforms.

The aspect of Carlos III's enlightened reign most pertinent to Moziño's study at Nootka is found in the Crown's patronage of science, from which resulted three major botanical surveys in the New World and the establishment of a royal institute of botany in Mexico City.[5] Factors influencing scientific activity during the late eighteenth century were rooted in the changing climate of European thought. The concept of naturalism—the assumption that the whole universe of mind and matter was guided and controlled by natural law—caused men to reassess their own countries. Ancient authority was no longer sufficient to establish the truth of long-accepted propositions; everything on earth, and even beyond, was submitted to questioning and new investigation. The age-old pursuit of riches gave way to a search for the physical and moral improvement of man, and a belief that knowledge and education could release the world's unexploited resources and set into motion a re-examination of the existing order.[6]

After the death of Carlos III, a number of Spain's scientific projects were carried to completion in the Americas, but the

[5] Alexander von Humboldt in *Ensayo Político sobre el Reino de la Nueva España*, edited by Juan A. Ortega y Medina (Mexico, D.F.: Editorial Porrua, 1966), p. 80: "Since the final years of the reign of Carlos III and during that of Carlos IV, the study of the natural sciences has made great progress not only in Mexico, but also in all of the Spanish colonies. No European government has sacrificed greater sums than has the Spanish in order to advance the knowledge of plants. Three botanical expeditions, those of Peru, New Granada, and New Spain, directed by [Hipólito] Ruiz and [José] Pavón, José Celestino Mutis, and Sessé and Mociño, have cost the State nearly 400,000 pesos. In addition, they have established botanical gardens in Manila and the Canary Islands."

[6] See Iris H. Wilson, "Spanish Scientists in the Pacific Northwest," in *Reflections of Western Historians*, edited by John A. Carroll (Tucson: University of Arizona Press, 1969), pp. 31–34.

ascension of Carlos IV to the Spanish throne in 1788 brought a general lack of governmental interest in the continuance of such studies. Unfortunately, circumstances accompanying the overall decline of Spain's power in the early nineteenth century prevented the realization of any plans for publication of scientific endeavors, and *Noticias de Nutka* was forced into relative obscurity.

The Nootka area of Vancouver Island has not, however, been overlooked in historical literature. Numerous studies have been published of the diplomatic complications and subsequent results of the Nootka Sound Controversy between Spain and England from 1789 to 1794. Since the Indian inhabitants of Nootka played only a supporting role in this well-known drama, they caused but slight concern on international levels. Their hopes and desires, except as they were related to supplying furs, were overshadowed by the commercial designs of the great European nations and the recently created United States.

Nevertheless, several of the early visitors to the Pacific Northwest were sufficiently interested in Nootka customs to make detailed observations of the daily lives and cultural traits of these natives. Some of the reports are surprisingly complete. Those left by the Spanish (at Nootka and elsewhere) are generally more extensive because of a pattern long established in New Spain quite unlike that of the British and Americans. The Spaniards from the first were dealing with large groups of Indians whom they intended to Christianize and incorporate fully into their empire as a source of labor and tribute. They often used the "ethnographic approach" (especially the clergy) in collecting information on native languages and culture. Most of these carefully compiled records are as yet in the form of unedited manuscripts.

In the eighteenth-century sense of natural science, *Noticias de Nutka* was perhaps the most "scientific" study made during the Spanish occupation of that area. Moziño, a kind of universal scholar, was formally trained in medicine, theology, and botany. He was among the first persons schooled in scientific methods to spend time at Nootka solely for purposes of observation. Although its circulation was limited, the *Noticias* was of immediate interest and use. Dr. Martín Sessé, director of the Royal Scientific Expedition to New Spain, proudly claimed that Moziño, during his stay in the Pacific Northwest, "not only discharged his duties in regard to natural history, but assembled notices of major importance to commerce and to the State which not one of the travelers encharged with exploring the island [of Nootka] had communicated to us. . . ." The doctor-naturalist had further, reported Sessé, "by the force of his ingenuity, learned the Nutkenese idiom in order to serve as an interpreter between his commander and the [local Indian] King Macuina. . . ."[7] A young man of great talent, Moziño typified the intellectual achievement of his age.

*Noticias de Nutka* was so well received by Moziño's contemporaries that Dionisio Alcalá Galiano, commander of the schooner *Sutil* on its visit to Nootka in 1792, declared that it was "preferable to study the accounts given by the distinguished Naturalist rather than rely upon one's own impressions." In his journal, Lieutenant Alcalá Galiano wrote:

> We are indebted to Mosiño for almost all the knowledge and accounts that we possess in regard to the inhabitants of Nootka. . . . The insight of this worthy subject, his perseverance, the intelligence by which he was able to acquire the Nootkan language, the intimate friendship which he gained with the most distinguished and most knowledgeable persons of the settlement, and his long residence with them are the reasons why our impartiality demands that we give preference to his investigations over our own.[8]

---

[7] Sessé to Viceroy Revilla Gigedo, Mexico, May 9, 1793, Archivo General de la Nación (Mexico, D.F.), Historia 527. This archive is hereafter cited as AGN.

[8] "Relación del Viaje hecho por las Goletas Sutil y Mexicana en el año de 1792 para reconocer el estrecho de Fuca," Museo Naval (Madrid), MS

Because Moziño's account was in part a history of Nootka Sound, it covered the multitude of visits to the area from the time of its discovery by the Spanish in 1774 through Bodega y Quadrás expedition of 1792. Considering the number of persons involved, *Noticias de Nutka* was surprisingly complete.

The first brief European contact with Nootka was made in 1774 by the Spaniard Juan Pérez, commander of an expedition instructed to explore the Pacific coast to 60° north latitude and take possession of those lands for Spain. Illness, fog, and contrary currents forced Pérez to turn his ship, the *Santiago*, southward short of his goal. Having reached a north latitude of 55°, the Spaniards coasted along the western shores of Queen Charlotte and Vancouver islands. Pérez did not land at Nootka, which he called San Lorenzo, but anchored offshore while 21 canoes containing nearly 150 amazed Indians approached his ship.[9] Moziño's account graphically portrays this unusual encounter:

> The sight of this ship at first filled the natives with terror, and even now [1792] they testify that they were seized with fright from the moment they saw on the horizon the giant "machine" which little by little approached their coasts. They believed that Qua-utz [the Creator] was coming to make a second visit, and were fearful that it was in order to punish the misdeeds of the people. As many as were able hid themselves in the mountains, others closed themselves up in their lodges, and the most daring

---

468, hereafter cited as "Relación del Viaje hecho por las Goletas Sutil y Mexicana." The Museo Naval is hereafter referred to as MN. See also José Espinosa y Tello, ed., *Relación del viaje hecho por las goletas Sutil y Mexicana en el año 1792* (Madrid: Imprenta Real, 1802; and Madrid: José Porrúa Turanzas, 1958), pp. 119–25.

9 "Viaje de la Navegación hecha por el Alferez Graduado D. Juan Pérez de ord. del Sr. Bucareli a la altura de los 55 grados donde está situada la entrada y Bahía de su nombre en la fragata *Santiago*, alias la *Nueva Galicia*, San Blas 3 de Noviembre de 1774," AGN, Historia 62; MN, MSS 331, 575 b's. See also Manuel P. Servín, "Instructions of Viceroy Bucareli to Ensign Juan Perez," *California Historical Society Quarterly*, XXXX (September, 1961), 239.

took their canoes out to examine more closely the huge mass that had come out of the ocean.[10]

Several of the more courageous Indians boarded the ship and took part in a friendly exchange of gifts. In addition, the natives pilfered some silver spoons which were found in their possession by Cook's expedition four years later.[11]

On his third voyage of exploration in 1778, the intrepid Captain James Cook entered Nootka with his two ships *Resolution* and *Discovery* and called the inlet King George's Sound. The Englishman later changed the name to Nootka, believing that to be the name used by the natives.[12] Anchoring at what Cook called Friendly Cove, the explorers remained in the sound for nearly a month. Cook's prolonged visit allowed him to describe the Indians and surrounding country in some detail. He also compiled a vocabulary of Nootkan words which served as a basis for subsequent studies of their language.[13]

John Ledyard of Connecticut, who sailed with Cook as a corporal of Marines on the *Resolution*, also wrote a narrative of the famous navigator's last expedition. Although called a "journal," the account was apparently compiled in 1783 after Ledyard's return to Hartford. The official record of the voyage by Captains Cook and James King did not appear in London until 1784. Ledyard's work devoted several pages to the Indians and their activities at Nootka and described the sale of beaver and other skins, which Cook's men had obtained from the natives for trink-

[10] See p. 66.
[11] Cook wrote: ". . . But what was most singular, two silver tablespoons were purchased from them, which, from their peculiar shape, were judged to be of Spanish manufacture. One of these strangers wore them round his neck by way of ornament" (M. B. Synge, ed., *Captain Cook's Voyages Round the World* [London: T. Nelson and Sons, 1897], p. 430; hereafter cited as Synge, ed., *Cook's Voyages*).
[12] See p. 67.
[13] Cook's description of Nootka and its inhabitants is found in his principal work, *A Voyage to the Pacific Ocean Undertaken by the Command of*

ets, for one hundred dollars apiece in China.[14] As a result, American merchants became interested in the possibilities of the Northwest fur trade.

By the beginning of the 1790's, enough accounts had been published of the fabulously profitable fur sale to focus worldwide attention on the Northwest Coast.[15] Consequently, the Nootka Indians were subjected to visits by a host of maritime traders, mainly British and American. Several of the men who had served with Cook, such as King, John Gore, Nathaniel Portlock, George Dixon, and George Vancouver later returned to the Pacific to become prominent explorers in their own right. The first trading voyage after the American Revolution was made by Captain John Hanna in 1785 from China to Nootka Sound. Reports of his profits brought at least five more British ships to the Northwest Coast in 1786.[16]

An informative account of the situation at Nootka Sound, although somewhat biased against the Spanish, is found in the journal of Captain John Meares, a former British naval officer

---

*His Majesty, for Making Discoveries in the Northern Hemisphere in the Years 1776, 1777, 1778, 1779, and 1780* (3 vols. and Atlas; London: G. Nicol and T. Cadell, 1784). Upon returning to the Sandwich [Hawaiian] Islands, which he had discovered, Cook was killed by natives on February 14, 1779. Volume III of Cook's work was written by Captain James King.

[14] James K. Munford, ed., *John Ledyard's Journal of Captain Cook's Last Voyage* (Corvallis: Oregon State University Press, 1963), Introduction by Sinclair H. Hitchings, pp. xxx–xlix, and pp. 69–76. In 1779, James King reported: "A few prime skins, which were clean and had been well preserved, were sold for one hundred and twenty [dollars] each" (quoted in Frederic W. Howay, ed., *The Dixon-Meares Controversy* [Toronto, Ont.: Ryerson Press, 1929], pp. 17–18).

[15] See Frederic W. Howay, "The Early Literature of the Northwest Coast," *Transactions of the Royal Society of Canada*, Vol. XVIII (May, 1924). Judge Howay's monumental editions of the letters and journals of many early participants in the Northwestern fur trade, e.g., John Meares, James Colnett, Nathaniel Portlock, George Dixon, and the American captains John Kendrick and Robert Gray of the *Columbia* and *Lady Washington*, respectively, give an excellent picture of the activity of this period.

[16] Hubert H. Bancroft, *History of the Northwest Coast* (San Francisco: The History Company, 1886), pp. 173–74; Howay, *The Dixon-Meares Controversy*, pp. 39–31.

turned trader-adventurer.[17] Because he did not have a special trading license for the Northwest Coast, as was required by the exclusive monopolies granted to the British South Sea Company and the East India Company, Meares evaded his government's restrictions by operating under the Portuguese flag. Early in 1788 he and a fellow Englishman, Captain William Douglas, commanded the Portuguese ships *Felice Adventurero* and *Iphigenia Nubiana* on an expedition from China to Nootka Sound. Meares put ashore some Chinese artisans with a supply of building materials in a small cove at Nootka in May, 1788, and then left on a trading cruise. The workers built a hut and the sloop *North West America*, the first of its kind constructed on that coast.[18]

The Spanish, who at that time claimed possession of the entire Pacific Northwest Coast as part of the Viceroyalty of New Spain, sent an expedition to Nootka under the command of First Pilot Don Esteban José Martínez in 1789. In a desire to strengthen Spanish interests, Martínez took formal possession of the port in June and established an outpost which he named Santa Cruz de Nutka. The new commandant attempted to maintain his nation's exclusive rights of ownership in the face of British, American, and French trading activities.[19]

Martínez' first act was the temporary arrest of Captain Douglas and the official Portuguese commander of the *Iphigenia*, Francisco

[17] John Meares, *Voyages Made in the Years 1788 and 1789 from China to the North West Coast of America* (London, 1790).

[18] John Meares, *The Memorial of John Mear[e]s to the House of Commons respecting the capture of vessels in Nootka Sound, [dated April 30, 1790, and presented May 13, 1790]*, edited by Nellie B. Pipes (Portland, Ore.: Metropolitan Press, 1933), pp. 2–3; hereafter cited as Meares, *Memorial*.

[19] "Copia de la orden instructiva comunicada al Alferez graduado de Navío Estevan José Martínez para su gobierno y observancia en la Ocupación del Puerto de San Lorenzo o Nutka," Archivo Histórico Nacional (Madrid), Estado 4289, hereafter cited as AHN; "Diario de la Navegación que Yo el Alferez de Navío de la Real Armada Dn. Estevan Josef Martínez voy a executar al Puerto de San Lorenzo de Nuca, mandando la Fragata Princesa, y Paquebot San Carlos de Orden de el Exmo. Sor. Dn. Manuel Antonio Florez, Virrey, Governador y Capitán general de N. España en el presente año de 1789," MN, MS 732. Martínez' diary, edited by Roberto Barreiro-Meiro, has

José Viana. These men were released with little difficulty, but Martínez then seized the *North West America* as security for money owed him by Meares's company for supplies furnished to the *Iphigenia*.[20] The subsequent arrival of Captain James Colnett in the *Argonaut*, with instructions from Meares to build a permanent factory at Nootka, brought about the final crisis. Colnett told Martínez that he was going to establish himself on land which Meares claimed to have purchased from the Nootka chief Maquinna.[21] In his *Noticias*, Moziño agreed that Martínez "of course had to oppose the demands which the Englishman haughtily set forth," but felt that the Spanish commandant had also insulted Colnett unnecessarily. "It is likely that the churlish nature of each one precipitated things up to this point, since those who sailed with both complained of them equally and condemned their uncultivated boorishness."[22]

Martínez ordered the arrest of Colnett, seized the *Argonaut* and its crew, and sent the ship, with the Englishmen as prisoners, to San Blas, Mexico. Shortly thereafter, another of Meares's ships, Captain Thomas Hudson's *Princess Royal*, was also seized and sent to San Blas.[23] Although Colnett was released and an agreement was made for the return of the *Princess Royal*,[24] which had been impressed into Spanish service, the events set into motion

---

been published as *[Diario de] Esteban José Martínez (1742–1798)* in Colección de Diarios y Relaciones para la Historia de los Viajes y Descubrimientos, Vol. VI (Madrid: Instituto Histórico de Marina, 1964); it is hereafter cited as Martínez, *Diario*.

[20] Henry R. Wagner, *Spanish Explorations in the Strait of Juan de Fuca* (Santa Ana, Tex.: Fine Arts Press, 1933), pp. 4–5; Martínez, *Diario*, May 31, 1789.

[21] Martínez, *Diario*, July 2 to July 14, 1789; Frederic W. Howay, ed., *The Journal of Captain James Colnett aboard the Argonaut from April 26, 1789, to November 3, 1791* (Toronto: The Champlain Society, 1940), pp. 53–131. Meares had formed a joint stock company, put Captains Thomas Hudson and James Colnett in command of the *Princess Royal* and *Argonaut*, respectively, and ordered them to Nootka to build a fort.

[22] See p. 74.

[23] Martínez, *Diario*, July 14, 1789.

[24] Howay, ed., *Journal of Captain James Colnett*, p. 135.

Noticias de Nutka

De su descubrimiento, situacion y producciones naturales: Sobre las constumbres de sus havitantes, Gobierno, Ritos, Cronologia, Ydioma, Musica, Poesia, Pesca, Caza, y Comercio de la Peleteria. Con la relacion de los Viajes hechos por los Europeos especialmente Españoles, y del convenio ajustado entre estos, y los Ingleses.

Añadese

Vn ensayo del Diccionario de la lengua de los Nutkeses, ilustrado todo con Laminas, por

D. Joseph Mariano Moziño Suarez de Figueroa Botánico Naturalista de la Real expedicion de nueva España, y de la de limites al Norte de California.

Año de 1793.

1. *Title page of "Noticias de Nutka" from the manuscript in Mexico City*

# Articulo 1.º

Del descubrimiento de Nutka ó Ysla de Mazarredo, su situacion temperamento, produciones naturales en general; talla, figura, adornos, trajes, y armas de sus habitantes.

La pequeña Ysla que en el dia conocemos con el nombre de Mazarredo, y en cuya Costa Oriental esta el fondeadero de Nutka, sin embargo de haver sido vista por el Piloto Español D. Juan Perez en el año de 1774, no comenzo á tener celebridad hasta el de 78, en que el infatigable Santiago Coock la reconocio, y hallo en ella abundan

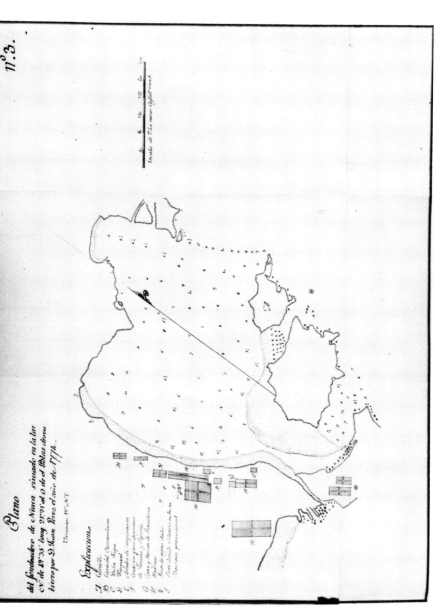

n.º 3.

Plano

del fondeadero de Nuca, situado en la lat
c.N de 49° 35´ long. 21° 21´ O de el Bolas descu
tierra por D. Juan Perez el año de 1774.

Varanor N° N°

Explicaciones

A   Canak.
B   Canak Ebrandiaco
C   Isla Legre
D   Varquad
E   salada de vaspineiro en
F   Guira y casa algunos
    de Guira y Agria
G   Casa y Maria de Candelera
G   Huertas
H   Plan de arena dulce
I   Ema Aumit Gilques.a ba su
J   Varias prominional

3.  Map of the anchorage of Nootka situated at 49° 35´ latitude north and
21° 21´ longitude west of San Blas discovered by Don Juan Pérez in the year 1772

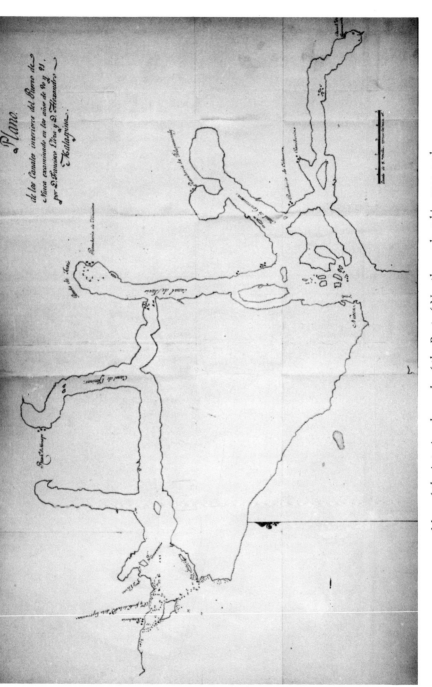

4. Map of the interior channels of the Port of Nootka explored in 1790 and
1791 by Don Francisco Eliza and Don Alejandro Malaspina

5.  *A Nootka* tais, *or chief*

6. *The wife of a Nootka chief*

7. *Nootka noblewoman with a child in the cradle*

*8. A Nootka commoner*

the controversy that would take the courts of Madrid and London five years to settle. Nootka Sound became the focal point of a full international crisis and thus the object of political as well as scientific investigation.

During these years several Americans were involved in the fur trade at Nootka. As Moziño commented in the *Noticias*, "The Americans, whose diligence sought to exceed that of their ancient progenitors, did not propose to be left without a part of this lucrative trade. [John] Kendrick left from Boston commanding the *Columbia Rediviva*, and [Robert] Gray, under his orders, commanding the sloop *Washington*."[25] These "Boston-men," as the Spanish called them, were considered disinterested bystanders during the crisis with the British because "their only purpose was trade." Moziño reported that the Americans "were able to establish such perfect harmony with the commandant of the port [Martínez] that even today [1792] they profess to be his most ardent friends. . . ."[26]

Several of the officers on these American vessels kept very complete records. The ship logs of Robert Haswell, John Hoskins, John Boit, and Joseph Ingraham give careful descriptions of the activities at Nootka and are informative sources concerning the Indians.[27] The relationship between the Americans and the Span-

[25] See p. 70.

[26] See p. 73. Martínez first encountered Kendrick inside Nootka Sound repairing the *Columbia* on May 6, 1789. The meeting was cordial, and Kendrick gave Martínez one of the commemorative medals of the Boston trading expedition, inscribed "Columbia and Washington commanded by J. Kendrick," to send to Viceroy Bucareli. Gray arrived in the *Washington* on June 17, and the friendship initiated by Kendrick and Martínez was maintained by the Americans throughout the Spanish controversy with the British during the summer and fall of 1789.

[27] Robert Haswell's logs of the *Columbia's* first and second voyages, John Hoskins' narrative of the second voyage, John Boit's log of the second voyage, and miscellaneous papers relating to the first and second voyages are found in Frederic W. Howay, ed., *Voyages of the "Columbia" to the Northwest Coast, 1787–90 and 1790–93* (Massachusetts Historical Society Collections, Vol. LXXIX; Cambridge, Mass.: Harvard University Press, 1941). Joseph Ingraham, who was second mate on the *Columbia* in 1789, returned to the Northwest as commander of the brigantine *Hope* from 1790 to 1792.

ish was extremely cordial, and the "Boston-men" were happy to cooperate in countering some of the claims made by the British of what had taken place in the controversy of 1789.[28]

Although the political and economic significance of Nootka Sound was a primary factor encouraging Spanish investigation of the Pacific Northwest during the last decades of the eighteenth century, the participants were motivated by other considerations as well. The spreading of the Catholic faith was always of primary importance in the frontier regions of New Spain, and by 1791 thirteen missions had been established from San Diego to San Francisco in Alta California. Six priests were at Nootka in 1789,[29] but plans for a mission never materialized. The excuse offered by the padres was a lack of cultivable land, but Moziño thought this to be a poor one indeed. "What a small obstacle! As if a mission and improved land were synonymous!"[30]

The wave of scientific interest spreading throughout Europe at this time continually carried new ideas into the Iberian Peninsula, and these in turn were transmitted to Spanish America. Carlos III had responded to the spirit of investigation by establishing a Royal Museum of Natural Science and Royal Botanical Garden in Madrid which also trained scientists for work at home and overseas. The system of nomenclature developed by the Swedish botanist Carolus Linnaeus (1707–78) inspired students to classify accordingly all the fauna and flora not just of the Old World but of the New as well. Spaniards studied the latest discoveries of French, English, and other foreign scholars in addition to reports

[28] The Americans of the *Columbia* and *Washington* had never been very friendly with the British after their first meeting with John Meares at Nootka on September 16, 1788. Haswell wrote in his log that Meares was doing his best to deceive them and was trying to prevent them from communicating with China. In 1792 Ingraham and Gray cooperated with Bodega y Quadra at Nootka and declared in writing that the British had not been dispossessed of any land or buildings by Martínez in 1789. See Bodega y Quadra, "Viaje de 1792," for a complete file of correspondence exchanged with Vancouver during this period.

[29] Howay, ed., *Journal of Captain James Colnett*, p. 61.

[30] See p. 85.

and new materials from the Indies to make complete and accurate collections. The unselfish exchange of scientific information among European countries, an admirable accomplishment in view of political and commercial rivalries of that day, enhanced the usefulness of individual studies.[31]

The Royal Scientific Expedition to New Spain of 1787 consisted of men educated in a tradition of accurate observation. Its members, and particularly Director Dr. Martín Sessé, were responsible for the establishment of a Royal Botanical Garden in Mexico City, the organization of surveys throughout the viceroyalty, and the training of a class of professional botanists. The Mexican-born José Moziño, author of *Noticias de Nutka*, was a graduate of the botanical institute founded by this group. Its professors and students participated in a number of scientific projects encouraged by the viceroys of New Spain during the 1790's. Even though handicapped by a lack of funds under Carlos IV, the Royal Scientific Expedition remained in Mexico until 1803.[32]

The Conde de Revilla Gigedo, viceroy of New Spain from 1789 to 1794, perhaps best carried on the enlightened tradition of Carlos III in the New World.[33] A capable administrator, Revilla Gigedo was vitally concerned about every aspect of the government and progress of his realm. He firmly believed in the value of scientific exploration and investigation and continually

[31] A good example of this "international cooperation" was the correlation of observations made of the transit of Venus in 1769. Results obtained by Captain Cook in Tahiti, by French and Spanish scientists in California, and by astronomers in China, Russia, and elsewhere were combined in calculating the distance from the earth to the sun.

[32] Iris H. Wilson, "Scientists in New Spain: The Eighteenth Century Expeditions," *Journal of the West*, I (July, 1962), 25–29.

[33] Juan Vicente de Güemes Pacheco de Padilla Horcasitas y Aguayo was the second Count of Revilla Gigedo to become viceroy of New Spain. His career has been recognized by many authorities as one of the most progressive during Mexico's final century. The viceroy achieved remarkable results in both domestic affairs and international relations. See Cayetano Alcázar Molina, *Historia de América y de los Pueblos Americanos: Los Virreinatos en el Siglo XVIII* (Barcelona: Editores Salvat, 1945).

offered his full support to Sessé's expeditions in all parts of Mexico. Further, the viceroy aided and encouraged special scientific projects such as the investigations of Don Antonio Pineda, chief of natural history on the around-the-world expedition of Alejandro Malaspina,[34] and the expedition of José Longinos Martínez to the Californias in 1792.[35]

Viceroy Revilla Gigedo reported to the Spanish minister Conde de Florida Blanca in 1791 that plans were being made for a new examination of the coasts of California and a final settlement of boundaries disputed by the English. He assured Florida Blanca that the proposed voyages "would without doubt give very exact accounts of all the coasts of California to 60° by amplifying and correcting the observations of Cook, the Count of La Pérouse[36] and other travelers." Revilla Gigedo also reminded the Spanish official that six expeditions had been organized during the two years of his term as viceroy (1789–91) and that these included

> ... that of Don Salvador Fidalgo in the packetboat *San Carlos* to Prince William [Sound]; that of Don Manuel Quimper to the Strait of [Juan de] Fuca in the sloop *Princesa Real*; that of Don Alejandro Malaspina in the two corvettes [*Descubierta* and

[34] Pineda spent from May to December, 1791, in the company of botanist Luis Neé and several artists making an intensive survey of the natural resources, fauna and flora, and native inhabitants of Mexico. See Iris H. Wilson, "Pineda's Report on the Beverages of New Spain," *Arizona and the West*, V (Spring, 1963), 79–90, and "Antonio Pineda y su viaje mundial," *Revista de Historia Militar*, VII (1964), 49–64.

[35] See Lesley Byrd Simpson, ed., *Journal of José Longinos Martínez: Notes and Observations of the Naturalist of the Botanical Expedition in Old and New California and the South Coast, 1791–1792* (San Francisco: John Howell-Books, 1961).

[36] Jean François Galaup, Comte de la Pérouse, sailed from Brest in August of 1785 as commander of a geographic, scientific, and commercial expedition around the world. The French enterprise spent a month along the Alaskan coast in the summer of 1786 and then sailed directly for Monterey, where the corps of scientists made copious notes on the Spanish province. The entire expedition was subsequently lost north of New Hebrides in 1788, but La Pérouse had previously forwarded installments of his journal to France. Se La Pérouse, *A Voyage around the World in the Years 1785, 1786, 1787 and 1788* (3 vols.; London: J. Johnson, 1799).

*Atrevida*] in search of the Strait of Ferrer Maldonado; that which is presently being carried out by Don Francisco Eliza in the packet-boat *San Carlos* and the small schooner *Santa Saturnina* through the Archipelago of Bucareli and the Strait of Fuca; that which will be undertaken immediately by Don Francisco Mourelle in the schooner *Mexicana*; and finally that which will be the final expedition under the command of Don Juan Francisco de la Bodega in the *Santa Gertrudis*, the *Princesa* and the schooner *Valdés*.[37]

The first two men, Salvador Fidalgo and Manuel Quimper, accompanied Lieutenant Francisco Eliza when he took over the post of Esteban Martínez as commandant of Nootka. Following instructions from Bodega y Quadra, head of the Naval Department of San Blas, Eliza dispatched Fidalgo on May 5, 1790, to explore the coast of Alaska in the *San Carlos*. Quimper was originally supposed to remain at Nootka with the *Princesa Real* (*Princess Royal*) for its delivery to Captain Colnett, but since the Englishmen had not arrived by the end of May,[38] Quimper set out with forty-one men to explore the Strait of Juan de Fuca. During the next two months he charted the coast on both the north and south sides of the strait as far as the San Juan Archipelago. Maintaining the scientific tradition of the period, Quimper made detailed notes on the plant and animal life.[39]

Commandant Eliza received further instructions for exploration from Bodega y Quadra when the *San Carlos* returned to Nootka from San Blas at the end of March, 1791. Viceroy Revilla Gigedo had ordered the expedition to "inspect those points which have not yet been well examined, with the view to form an exact general plan of the whole coast." The principal areas to

[37] Revilla Gigedo to Florida Blanca, Mexico, November 12, 1791, Archivo General de Indias (Sevilla), Estado 20; this archive is hereafter cited as AGI.

[38] Colnett did not reach Nootka until the following September (Howay, ed., *Journal of Captain Colnett*, p. 180).

[39] Michael E. Thurman, *The Naval Department of San Blas: New Spain's Bastion for Alta California and Nootka, 1767–1798* (Glendale, Calif.: The Arthur H. Clark Company, 1967), pp. 312–16. Quimper's journal of his voyage in the *Princesa Real* is included in Wagner, *Spanish Explorations in the Strait of Juan de Fuca*, pp. 82–136.

be touched upon from Mount St. Elias in the north to Trinidad in the south were Bucareli Inlet, Straits of Font and Heceta, bays of San Rafael and Carrasco, Port of Clayoquot, and the inside of the Strait of Juan de Fuca.[40]

Leaving the port of Nootka under the command of Pedro de Alberni, captain of the Company of Catalonian Volunteers, Eliza set out in the *San Carlos*, accompanied by the schooner *Santa Saturnina*. Although instructed to do so,[41] Eliza did not give any detailed description of the animals, birds, and fish found in the strait because Quimper had described them the year before. His first pilot Juan Pantoja, however, recorded his own scientific observations and made notes on the natural resources and Indian life of the region.[42]

The most comprehensive Spanish exploring expedition of the period, the sixty-two-month around-the-world expedition of Alejandro Malaspina, reached the Northwest Coast at Mulgrave Sound, Lituya Bay, Alaska, in the summer of 1791. The two corvettes, *Descubierta* and *Atrevida*, commanded by Malaspina and José Bustamante y Guerra, respectively, had been built especially for scientific investigation and were staffed with personnel hand-picked for their ability in navigation, cartography, astronomy, natural history, and artistic reproduction. The Spanish Minister of Marine, Antonio Valdés, had spared nothing to insure the success of a voyage that would rival those of Cook and La Pérouse.[43]

[40] Bodega y Quadra to Francisco Eliza, "Instrucciones secretas," February 4, 1791, AGN, Historia 69. On Joseph Ingram's map the Strait of Font apparently represents the entrance to Portland Canal or Revilla Gigedo Channel or perhaps both.

[41] Article IV directed Eliza to examine carefully "the nature and character of the country, the animals, insects, birds, fish, metals, precious stones, plants, vegetables, and fruits . . . " (*ibid.*).

[42] Extracto de la navegación que ha hecho el piloto Don Juan Pantoja y Arriaga en el piloto Don Juan Pantoja y Arriaga en el paquebot de S. M. el San Carlos . . . desde San Blas el 4 de Febrero de 1791," MN, MS 271.

[43] "Plan de un Viaje Científico y Político al Rededor del Mundo Remitido

## Introduction

The Malaspina expedition arrived at Nootka Sound on August 12 and spent two weeks inspecting the Spanish installation, gaining the friendship of Chief Maquinna, and seeking whatever information Viceroy Revilla Gigedo might find helpful in negotiating settlement of the controversy between Spain and England. The artists sketched local Indians and their cultural activities while the naturalist, Austrian-born Tadeo Haenke, gathered samples of the fauna and flora.[44] When appropriate maps had been collected and prepared, and observations of the surrounding area completed, the group set sail for the port of Monterey, capital of Alta California.[45]

The fifth expedition mentioned in Viceroy Revilla Gigedo's letter to Florida Blanca was that proposed for Lieutenant Francisco Antonio Mourelle in the schooner *Mexicana*. Like commanders of previous voyages, Mourelle was instructed to make friends with the Indians, look for European establishments, take possession of new areas, discover any valuable metals or precious stones, and ascertain what animals the natives had, what the wild ones were, what kinds of fish the sea held, and what classes of birds lived in the forests.[46] In addition, Mourelle's expedition was

---

a el Exmo. Sr. Bailio Fray Antonio Valdés de Madrid en Sept. 10 de 1788," MN, MS 316; Pedro de Novo y Colson, *La Vuelta al Mundo por las Corbetas Descubierta y Atrevida al Mando del Capitán de Navío D. Alejandro Malaspina desde 1789 a 1794* (Madrid: Depósito Hidrográfico, 1885). The career of Malaspina is summarized in "Antiguedades de los oficiales de guerra de la Armada," MN, MS 1161 bis. His expedition did not actually circumnavigate the globe, but returned from the Philippines, Australia, and New Zealand by way of South America.

[44] The diary and illustrations of artist Tomás de Suría are found in the Malaspina Papers, Beinecke Collection, Yale University Library; Haenke's observations are scattered in numerous archives of Europe. See Josef Kuhnel, *Thaddaeus Haenke, Leben und Wirken eines Forschers* (Prague, 1960).

[45] See Donald C. Cutter, *Malaspina in California* (San Francisco: John Howell-Books, 1960).

[46] Revilla Gigedo to Mourelle, "Instrucción reservada que ha de observar el Teniente de Fragata de la Real Armada Dn. Francisco Antonio Mourelle en el viaje a que está destinado a la costa de California en la Goleta Mexicana," Mexico, September 9, 1791, AHN, Estado 4289. Mourelle was second

to precede Bodega y Quadra's meeting with the English to ascertain which place on the south coast was best adaptable to Spanish settlement when the terms of the Nootka Convention were put into effect.[47]

The *Mexicana* was ready to sail in December of 1791, but Mourelle could not depart because of sickness. Malaspina, who had returned to Acapulco, suggested that two of his top officers, Dionisio Alcalá Galiano and Cayetano Valdés, take over command of the expedition in two schooners, the *Mexicana* and another just like it, the *Sutil*. The viceroy accepted the proposal, and Malaspina instructed a portion of his officers and crew to prepare for arrival of their new ships in Acapulco. Owing to several delays, the expedition did not depart until March, 1792, reaching Nootka a month after Bodega y Quadra had taken command of that port. Mourelle's project of looking for a new port was set aside, and Alcalá Galiano and Valdés followed a plan similar to the Malaspina effort.[48]

The *Sutil* and *Mexicana* left Nootka on June 5, 1792, and reached Nuñez Gaona (Neah Bay) the following day. Here they found the *Princesa Real* anchored in the cove and Salvador Fidalgo scouting the shore.[49] Several days later Alcalá Galiano and Valdés proceeded into the straits of Juan de Fuca and Rosario, noting the small islands and inlets. After leaving Bellingham Bay, the Spaniards encountered the English vessels *Discovery* and *Chatham* under the command of Captain George Vancouver, the commissioner sent to carry out the terms of the Nootka Con-

---

in command to Bodega y Quadra on the *Sonora* to 55° north latitude in 1775 and second again to Bodega y Quadra on board the *Princesa* which reached 61° north latitude in 1779.

[47] Wagner, *Spanish Explorations in the Strait of Juan de Fuca*, p. 46.

[48] *Ibid.*, pp. 47–58; "Relación del Viaje hecho por las Goletas Sutil y Mexicana."

[49] Fidalgo had set up some provincial buildings, made friends with the Indians, and was proceeding with plans for a permanent Spanish establishment. This final act of expansion was short-lived since the port was abandoned in September, 1792, with Fidalgo's return to Nootka.

vention. Alcalá Galiano informed Vancouver that the Spanish commandant, Juan Francisco de la Bodega y Quadra, was awaiting the Englishman's arrival at Nootka Sound.[50]

Alcalá Galiano and Vancouver cordially exchanged results of their respective explorations in the strait and agreed to continue together. The *Discovery* and *Chatham* left their anchorage at Birch Bay and joined the Spanish vessels for a short time, but relations became strained when the British appeared to distrust the Spanish survey. Parting company with Alcalá Galiano and Valdés, Vancouver sent a message of his position overland by some Indians to Bodega y Quadra, proceeded up Johnstone Strait, and finally emerged into the open waters of Queen Charlotte Sound. After a brief exploration northward, the ships headed for Nootka; first the *Chatham* and then the *Discovery* anchored in Friendly Cove on August 28. The *Sutil* and *Mexicana*, sailing close to the Vancouver Island shore through Goletas channel, entered the Pacific several days after the British and reached Nootka Sound on August 30.[51]

The arrival of Vancouver at Nootka in 1792 brought the problems between Spain and England again into focus. The convention signed between the two countries on October 28, 1790, had resulted from difficult negotiations. The British public wanted revenge for the alleged insult to their sovereignty caused by the actions of Martínez in seizing British vessels and officers. Merchants demanded the undisputed right to send British traders to the area. Spain, on the other hand, claimed possession of the Pacific Northwest under the papal bull of Alexander VI in 1493, and pointed to their occupation of Nootka. The Spanish wanted to retain the Northwest Coast mainly because they feared other European settlements would endanger their establishments far-

[50] "Relación del Viaje hecho por las Goletas Sutil y Mexicana."
[51] See Edmond S. Meany, *Vancouver's Discovery of Puget Sound* (New York: The Macmillan Company, 1907), and Bern Anderson, *The Life and Voyages of Captain George Vancouver* (Seattle: University of Washington Press, 1960), pp. 90–97.

ther south. Great Britain's strength, however, gave it the upper hand, and the Spanish practically abandoned their claim of exclusive sovereignty.[52]

Royal orders for implementing the terms of the Nootka agreement reached Revilla Gigedo in the spring of 1791. The viceroy, in accordance with the Crown's suggestion, appointed Bodega y Quadra, commandant of the Naval Department of San Blas, as the Spanish commissioner. He received his instructions in Revilla Gigedo's letter of October 29, 1791.[53]

The Spanish were to return to the British any property Martínez had seized in 1789. When this had been done, Spain was free to maintain a post at Nootka, but Revilla Gigedo favored abandoning the area to the English and building a new Spanish settlement on the north side of the Strait of Juan de Fuca. The viceroy also recommended that the strait be made the northern boundary of exclusive Spanish ownership instead of the forty-eighth parallel mentioned in the royal orders. Another boundary running due north from the strait to latitude 60° north would assure the inclusion of any territories in the province of New Mexico.[54]

Bodega y Quadra was the logical person to carry out the terms of the Nootka Convention. A seasoned navigator and veteran of previous expeditions to the Pacific Northwest, the senior naval officer enjoyed the utmost confidence of Viceroy Revilla Gigedo and was often singled out for his skillful rendering of charts and plans. Bodega y Quadra's advancement in the royal service was

[52] A thorough study of these negotiations is found in William R. Manning, "The Nootka Sound Controversy," *American Historical Association Annual Report of 1904* (Washington, D. C.: U. S. Government Printing Office, 1905), pp. 279–478. According to the terms of the convention both Spanish and British ships could have free entry into any port north of the Spanish settlements, and British subjects could not form any establishments on coasts of the Americas occupied by Spain.

[53] Revilla Gigedo to Juan Francisco de la Bodega y Quadra, Mexico, October 29, 1791, AHN, Estado 4287; AGN, Historia 67.

[54] Wagner, *Spanish Exploration in the Strait of Juan de Fuca*, pp. 60, 62.

particularly rapid for a person born in the New World. His family, which had settled in Lima, Peru, was of Basque origin, and his father, a minor noble, was alcalde *in absentia* of the Valley of Somorrostro in northern Spain.[55] Their second son, Juan Francisco, entered the navy at the age of nineteen, was trained at Cádiz and commissioned on October 12, 1767.[56]

As a lieutenant, Bodega y Quadra commanded the thirty-six-foot schooner *Sonora* as consort to the expedition of Bruno de Heceta from San Blas to the Northwest Coast in 1775.[57] On the third major Spanish expedition to the northern area in 1779, Bodega y Quadra, commanding the frigate *Favorita* in the company of Lieutenant Ignacio de Arteaga and the *Princesa*, reached Alaska and the Bering Sea in 61° north latitude.[58] The successful navigator, praised for his resourcefulness, was awarded the Cross of the Order of Santiago while serving in Spain. Bodega y Quadra was promoted to captain and received his appointment as commandant of the department of San Blas in time to accompany

---

[55] Bodega y Quadra's parents were Tomás de la Bodega y de las Llanas of Vizcaya, Spain, and Francisca de Mollinedo y Losada, a native of Lima, Peru, whose parents were from Bilbao. The name Quadra came from Juan Francisco's paternal grandmother, Isabel de la Quadra. By arrangement with his relative and sponsor in Peru, Antonio de la Quadra, he added Quadra as a second last name to honor this branch of the family. Although the British and others, including at times Bodega y Quadra himself, used only the Quadra portion of his name, it is not technically correct that it should stand alone. See Donald C. Cutter, "California, Training Ground for Spanish Naval Heroes," *California Historical Society Quarterly*, XL (June, 1961), 115.

[56] "Oficiales Asuntos Particulares," MN, MS 1163.

[57] "Navegación hecha por don Juan Francisco de la Bodega y Quadra, Teniente de Fragata de la Real Armada y Comandante de la Goleta Sonora, a los descubrimientos de los Mares y Costa Septentrional de California," MN, MS 622; "Segunda Exploración de la Costa Septentrional de la California en 1775 con la Fragata Santiago y Goleta Sonora, mandado por el Teniente de Navío D. Bruno de Heceta y de Fragata D. Juan de la [Bodega y] Quadra desde el Puerto de San Blas hasta los de latitud," MN, MS 331.

[58] "Tercera exploración de la Costa Septentrional de Californias con las dos Fragatas Princesa y Faborita, mandadas por el Teniente de Navío D. Ignacio Arteaga, y por el de la misma clase D. Juan de la [Bodega y] Quadra en el año de 79 desde el Puerto de San Blas hasta los 61 grados de latitud," MN, MS 331.

Viceroy Revilla Gigedo to Mexico in 1789. He served at San Blas until his death in the spring of 1794.[59]

Bodega y Quadra's expedition "of the Limits to the North of California" in 1792 to settle the Nootka claims was intended to resolve finally all difficulties with England over territorial rights. It was also the last major Spanish effort to make a full investigation of the northern area. For this reason, Viceroy Revilla Gigedo's appointment of José Mariano Moziño to accompany Bodega y Quadra at Nootka was opportune. Moziño filled the position of "botanist-naturalist" and was given the assistance of two companions from the Royal Scientific Expedition of New Spain: José Maldonado, an anatomist[60] as well as a botanist, and Atanasio Echeverría, a botanical artist. Moziño's efforts on this expedition, which departed from San Blas on March 3, 1792, resulted in his preparation of the *Noticias de Nutka* translated herein.

Revilla Gigedo chose Moziño to make the scientific study at Nootka primarily because of his tireless contributions to the royal expedition in Mexico.[61] Like Bodega y Quadra, Moziño was a Creole, having been born in the Mexican pueblo of Temas-

[59] The career of Bodega y Quadra is treated in Thurman, *The Naval Department of San Blas,* and in Marcial Gutiérrez Camarena, *San Blas y las Californias* (Mexico, D.F.: Editorial Jus., 1956).

[60] Maldonado later accompanied the expedition of Lieutenant Jacinto Caamaño in the *Aránzazu* for a little more than a month exploring the coastal regions to the north as far as Bucareli Inlet. Maldonado recorded observations of plants and animals. Caamaño's journal is contained in "Extracto del Diario de las navegaciones, exploraciones y descubrimientos hechos en la América Septentrional por D. Jacinto Caamaño," Archivo del Ministerio de Asuntos Exteriores (Madrid), MS 10; this archive is hereafter cited as AMAE. See also "The Journal of Don Jacinto Caamaño," edited by Henry R. Wagner and W. A. Newcombe and translated by Captain Harold Grenfell in the *British Columbia Historical Quarterly,* II (July–October, 1938), 189–222, 265–301.

[61] The viceroy had early been cognizant of Moziño's ability and approved his employment, with that of José Maldonado, as an official member of the expedition. A shortage of funds made it difficult to keep the new men on the payroll, especially when the viceroy's petition for additional support was unrealistically denied by Carlos IV (Orden del Rey Carlos IV, [1792], 4ª División, Legajo No. 15, Archivo del Jardín Botánico [Madrid]). The appoint-

caltepec in 1757. His parents were both of pure Spanish blood.[62] Moziño was educated in his native pueblo until 1774, when he entered the Seminario Tridentino in Mexico City. His progress was so outstanding that in just two years he received a degree of Bachelor of Philosophy. In 1778, still only twenty years old, Moziño was awarded an academic degree in scholastic theology and ethics.[63]

Sometime in 1778, Moziño married Doña María Rita Rivera y Melo Montaño and moved with his bride to Oaxaca, where he began his first career as a professor of ecclesiastical history, theology, and ethics at the seminary. He became dissatisfied with the provincial college atmosphere, however, and in 1784 returned to Mexico to enroll in the university school of medicine. His wife disapproved of the move and remained in Oaxaca, where she later complained that Moziño had abandoned her without support.[64]

While completing his studies in medicine at the Royal and Pontifical University of Mexico in 1786 and 1787, Moziño also attended the Royal Academy of San Carlos, taking a two-year

---

ment of Moziño and Maldonado to accompany Bodega y Quadra afforded Revilla Gigedo an excellent temporary solution for his dilemma.

[62] A baptismal certificate signed by Br. Juan Antonio Cardoso stating that "En veinte y quatro de Septiembre de mil setesientos sinquenta y siete años [September 24, 1757] *Venia Parochi* Baptisé solemnemente, y puse los santos oleos a Jph. Mariano Español, Hijo Lexitimo de Lexitimo matrimonio de Dn. Juan Antonio Mosiño y de Da. Manuela Losada . . . ," and testimony of certain residents of Temascaltepec affirming that Moziño's parents were "cristianos biejos, sin mezcla en la sangre, ni infamia en linaje," are contained in "Información de legitimidad y limpieza de vida y costumbres de Don Jsph Mariano Moziño natural del Rl. y minas de Temascaltepec—para vestir manto y Beca de Colexial en este Seminario," MS in the archives of the University of Mexico, quoted in Alberto B. Carreño, ed., *Noticias de Nutka* (Mexico, D.F.: Sociedad Mexicana de Geografía y Estadística, 1913), pp. vi–viii.

[63] Carreño, ed., *Noticias de Nutka*, pp. vi ff.

[64] Bishop José Gregorio to Doña María Rita Rivera, Oaxaca, August 14, 1790, AGN, Historia 465. The bishop agreed with María that Moziño had "little more to lean on than his great God-given talent and ability for writing." Moziño always maintained that his wife had left him of her own accord.

course in mathematics given by Engineer Miguel Costanzó of the Royal Army. A diligent and capable student, Moziño was able, at the same time, to be number one in his class at the academy,[65] teach mathematics at the university,[66] and double up on his medical studies. On the basis of an oral examination, he finished his third year in medicine in six months and was allowed to enroll in his fourth on October 19, 1786. He received the degree of Bachelor in Medicine on April 30, 1787.[67]

Instead of following the medical career for which he was prepared, Moziño was attracted by research, particularly in the field of medicinal plants, and thus he enrolled in the course in botany at the Royal Botanical Garden in Mexico City. At the graduation exercises in 1789, Moziño, recognized as the outstanding student of the year, was selected to deliver the opening address. The former theology professor chose to defend the Linnaean system of botanical nomenclature, illustrating its significance in the scientific world.[68]

Director Martín Sessé of the Royal Scientific Expedition to New Spain quickly became aware of Moziño's ability. He invited the newly qualified botanist to work with the Spanish scientists then engaged in collecting and classifying the flora of Mexico. Sessé's commission was to identify, classify, and reproduce pictorially all new plant species throughout the viceroyalty. His three official botanists needed additional assistants for such an immense undertaking, and thus Moziño and his classmate José Maldonado joined the royal expedition. From 1790 to 1792 they took part in excursions throughout the region northwest of

[65] "Certificado extendido por el Ingeniero Costanzó," Mexico, August 27, 1793, Archives of the Real Academia Nacional de Medicina de Madrid, Carpeta 65, quoted in Juan Carlos Arias Divita, *Las Expediciones Científicas Españolas durante el siglo XVIII* (Madrid: Ediciones Cultura Hispánica, 1968), p. 37.

[66] The "Certificado de la Real y Pontifica Universidad de Mexico," Mexico, October 19, 1793 (*ibid.*), showed that Moziño substituted in the chair of astrology and mathematics from May 2 to September 7, 1786.

[67] *Ibid.*, p. 36; Carreño, ed., *Noticias de Nutka*, p. xv.

[68] *Gazeta de Mexico*, III (December 22, 1789), 439.

Mexico City in the course of which hundreds of species of plants were collected and named.[69]

While on an expedition near Aguascalientes, Moziño received word from Sessé that Viceroy Revilla Gigedo had ordered that "José Moziño, Josef Maldonado, and the best of the artists" should immediately join the expedition of Juan Francisco de la Bodega y Quadra which was about to depart from San Blas to survey the northern limits of California.[70] Moziño was then accompanied by the "best artist," Atanasio Echeverría, so the two men set out for San Blas, where they were joined by Maldonado. The three were welcomed by Bodega y Quadra; and with the departure of the vessels *Activo* and *Santa Gertrudis* they became part of the historic voyage.[71]

The expedition arrived in Nootka Sound on April 29, 1792, and remained until the following September. The duration of Bodega y Quadra's stay allowed Moziño sufficient time to compile the information and vocabulary included in the *Noticias* and also to gather and classify, with Maldonado, more than two hundred species of plants, animals, and birds according to the Linnaean system.[72] The artist Echeverría sketched general scenes and made numerous botanical and zoological plates to accompany Moziño's descriptions. Archibald Menzies, the Scottish botanist accompanying Vancouver's expedition, admired the results of their work, and the men exchanged notes on various plants.[73]

[69] "Testimonio del Expediente sobre haberse resuelto que el Botánico Don Jaime Senseve quede en Mexico y que en su lugar salga con la Expedición el Médico Dn. José Mosiño, nombrado para la disección de los animales al Cirujano Maldonado," Archivo del Museo de Ciencias Naturales, Flora Española—Año 1790. This archive is hereafter cited as AMCN.

[70] Sessé to Revilla Gigedo, Mexico, May 9, 1793, AGN, Historia 527.

[71] Bodega y Quadra, "Viaje de 1792."

[72] Accurate identification was difficult because the works of Linnaeus were based upon European species. Moziño's list is contained in the "Catálogo de los Animales y Plantas que han reconocido y determinado según el sistema de Linneo los Facultativos de mi Expedición Don José Moziño y Don José Maldonado," AMAE, MS 145. See Appendix B, in this volume.

[73] Menzies commented in his journal that Moziño, Maldonado, and Echeverría "were part of a Society of Naturalists who were employed of

Moziño and Echeverría, after a two-month stay in Monterey, California, arrived in San Blas on February 2, 1793.[74] They proceeded directly to the Mexican capital,[75] where they rejoined members of the Royal Scientific Expedition and began to put their notes and drawings in order. Moziño completed a copy of his "Noticias de Nutka," which he delivered to Viceroy Revilla Gigedo before April 20, 1793, when he left on an expedition to southern Mexico.[76] Apparently Echeverría placed his original sketches in the hands of fellow artists at the Academy of San Carlos for multiple reproduction. The extant drawings are not those bearing Echeverría's signature, but contemporary copies.[77] Sometime in the spring of 1793, the artist rejoined Moziño in the south and the two men journeyed to investigate the erupting volcano of San Andrés de Tuxtla.[78]

---

late years in examining Mexico and New Spain for the purpose of collecting materials for a Flora Mexicana which they said would soon be published, and with the assistance of so good an artist it must be a valuable acquisition" (*Menzies' Journal of Vancouver's Voyage April to October, 1792,* edited by C. F. Newcombe [Victoria, B.C.: W. H. Cullin, 1923]).

[74] Sessé to Revilla Gigedo, Mexico, May 9, 1793, AGN, Historia 527.

[75] Under orders from Bodega y Quadra, Moziño accompanied the English Captain Robert Broughton (returning to England at the request of Vancouver) to Mexico City.

[76] Sessé to Revilla Gigedo, Mexico, May 9, 1793, AGN, Historia 527.

[77] "Planos geográficos y dibujos para ilustrar el Diario de D. Juan Francisco de la Bodega y Quadra," AMAE, MS 146; Revilla Gigedo Papers, Vol. XXIX, Private Collection of Irving W. Robbins, Atherton, California. The two sets of drawings were completed by the following artists: Tomás Suría, José Cardero, Gabriel Gil, Julian Marchena, José Gutiérrez, J. Vicente de la Cerda, José María Montés de Oca, Francisco Lindo, José María Guerrero, José María Vásquez, M. Garcia, José Castañeda Mendoza, Nicolas Moncayo, José Mariano de Aguila, Miguel Albian, and Manuel López. Both Tomás Suría and José Cardero had been with Malaspina at Nootka in 1791 and Cardero returned there with the Alcalá Galiano—Valdés expedition in 1792. Several of the remaining artists, especially Vincente de la Cerda and Francisco Lindo, worked with the Royal Scientific Expedition in New Spain.

[78] Moziño to Revilla Gigedo, San Andrés de Tuxtla, November 27, 1793, AGN, Historia 558. Echeverría apparently had trouble completing work already begun and caused Sessé, at the time of the artist's departure for Cuba in 1798, to complain: "[Echeverría] shut his ears to my comments and

Today Moziño's study of Nootka Sound is cited in works concerning the Northwest Coast and its inhabitants, but few people are aware of its comprehensive nature. The world-renowned naturalist Baron Alexander von Humboldt was so impressed with the *Noticias* on his visit to Mexico in 1803 that he made copious notes from a copy of Moziño's manuscript at the Royal Botanical Garden.[79] "Despite the exact accounts which we owe to the English and French navigators," wrote Humboldt, "it would be very interesting to publish in French the observations which Moziño has made about the customs of the natives of Nootka, because they include a great number of curious facts." Humboldt gave the following examples:

> . . . The union of civil and religious power in the person of the prince or Tais; the struggle between the powers of good and evil which govern the world, that is, between Quautz and Matlox; the origin of the human race in an epoch in which deer lacked antlers, birds wings, and dogs tails; the [Legend of the] Eve of the Nootkans, who lived alone in the flowered forest of Yuquatl when the God Quautz, navigating in a copper canoe, came to visit her; the education of the first man . . . the genealogy of the nobility of Nootka . . . the calendar of Nootkans, which begins the year in the summer solstice . . . etc. etc.[80]

José Moziño drew upon his varied educational background, as well as his normally inquisitive nature, to produce a work of overall interest. His awareness of the political situation with England prompted him to comment on Spain's future in the Pacific Northwest. Moziño's conclusion that the Spanish should

---

his eyes to the state of his sketches" (Sessé to Branciforte, Mexico, November 18, 1798, AGN, Historia 465).

[79] Humboldt, *Ensayo Político*, pp. 81, 212, noted that the "distinguished doctor, José Moziño," and "Señor Echeverría, painter of plants and animals and whose works can compete with the most perfect which Europe has produced of this class [of artist], were both born in New Spain and both occupy a very distinguished place among learned persons and artists without having left their native country."

[80] *Ibid.*, p. 215.

withdraw from Nootka illustrates unusual insight. He was firmly convinced that retention of the establishment by Spain offered no possible advantage to the Crown for either military or commercial purposes. Moziño warned: "Anyone can see that six or eight thousand men would scarcely be enough to guard the area, and that, even if we took exclusive possession of the fur trade, it probably would not defray the enormous expense which our defense would require."[81]

On the other hand, Moziño was favorably impressed with California. "There our conquest has taken roots, our religion has been propagated, and our hopes are greatest for obtaining obvious advantages to benefit all the monarchy." He also recommended that individual Spaniards be encouraged to enter the fur trade because of the availability of Indian trade goods within the empire. Moziño predicted:

> One active trader can make at least two trips every three years and realize a minimum of 300 percent on each one of them despite the reduction which the initial price of sea otters has suffered and the frequent restrictions of the emperor of China. . . . As the Spanish traders along the coast increase in number, necessity itself will make the English and other foreigners retire. In this way, by reaping benefits instead of incurring expenses, we will succeed in securing our possessions and bringing about happiness and prosperity.[82]

Moziño's optimism about the future of Spain and the fur trade was somewhat misplaced, but his recommendation for abandonment of Nootka coincided with Viceroy Revilla Gigedo's opinion of 1791 which was again expressed in a report to Madrid on April 12, 1793.[83]

The attempt of Bodega y Quadra to settle the controversy with

[81] See p. 93.
[82] See p. 97.
[83] Revilla Gigedo to Duque de Alcudia, Mexico, April 12, 1793, Revilla Gigedo Papers, Volume XIII, Private Collection of Irving W. Robbins, Atherton, California.

England was a failure. When the two commanders met, Vancouver maintained that his instructions were to receive all of Nootka, whereas the Spanish commissioner asserted that the return of the land where John Meares had built his hut in 1788 was the most that the terms of the Nootka Convention required. Despite a most cordial relationship based upon mutual admiration and respect, Bodega y Quadra and Vancouver reached a stalemate and could agree only to refer the matter back to Madrid and London.[84]

Bodega y Quadra sailed for California on September 22, 1792, stopping shortly at Neah Bay to order Salvador Fidalgo's return to Nootka as commandant. Vancouver remained at Friendly Cove completing his surveys until the middle of October, when he set sail to join Bodega y Quadra in Monterey. The five-year Nootka Sound Controversy was finally terminated by an agreement signed at Madrid on January 11, 1794, by the Baron of St. Helens for Great Britain and the Duke of Alcudia for Spain. Free access to Nootka was thereby guaranteed to both nations, and the Spanish evacuated the infamous northern port on April 2, 1795.[85]

José Moziño worked with the Royal Scientific Expedition in Mexico, Guatemala, and the West Indies until 1803, when he accompanied Director Sessé to Madrid. At this time Carlos IV, a poor successor to his father's greatness, showed little effective interest in projects of natural history and offered the returning scientists no means for publication of the expedition's reports. Events of greater urgency were commanding the Spanish monarch's attention. Moziño rightly feared that, unless he were allowed to continue his commission, "the precious collection" which had been the fruit of his "long and difficult voyages . . . and which could be of such honor and utility to the nation"

[84] Bodega y Quadra, "Viaje de 1792;" Anderson, *Life and Voyages of George Vancouver*, pp. 100–19.
[85] Florian Guest, "The Establishment of the Villa de Branciforte," *California Historical Society Quarterly*, XLI (March, 1962), 30.

would be lost.[86] He asked that Echeverría, who had "skill in the herbariums, animal specimens, drawings, and manuscripts," be assigned to help him complete the work which, above all, would "manifest to Europe that Spain had not been careless in making investigations of its vast dominions of both Americas by persons instructed in natural history."[87]

During the fall of 1808, French forces invaded the Spanish peninsula and Napoleon placed Joseph Bonaparte on the throne which Carlos IV had abdicated the previous March in favor of his son Fernando VII. Ironically, French occupation of Madrid brought Moziño unexpected help. Napoleon's brother, intrigued by the New World collections, appointed Moziño director of the Royal Museum of Natural History and professor of zoology at the Royal Academy of Medicine.[88] These favors, however, proved to be the Mexican scientist's downfall. When the French withdrew from Madrid in 1812, he was considered a traitor and temporarily arrested by the victorious Spanish patriots.

The final events of Moziño's life brought a sad ending to his colorful and productive career.[89] Forced to flee on foot to the French border, he placed his personal manuscripts, drawings, and herbaria in an old handcart and eventually reached Montpellier with only a portion of his possessions still intact. There Moziño met the Swiss scientist Augustin-Pyramus de Candolle, who was

[86] Moziño to Pedro Cevallos, Madrid, October 24, 1808, ACMN, Flora Española—Año 1808. In this letter Moziño also reports the death of Sessé and proposes that the materials be turned over to the government for disposition to the Museum of Natural Science and the Royal Botanical Garden.

[87] *Ibid.* Although Moziño's pleas for aid fell upon deaf ears, Echeverría, returning to Spain from service in Cuba in 1802, had received an appointment in 1804 as Second Director of Painting at the Royal Academy of San Carlos in Mexico. Through influence at court, Echeverría began collecting his salary at once, pending his departure for Mexico. He continued in Madrid until 1808 when the French invasion forced him to flee with his family to Seville; he was still in southern Spain in 1811.

[88] Juan A. Ortega, editor of Humboldt's *Ensayo Político*, notes (p. 96) that Moziño served four times as president of the Academy of Medicine as well.

[89] These are well told by Harold W. Rickett, "The Royal Botanical Expedition to New Spain," *Chronica Botanica*, XI (1947), 77–79.

then lecturing in botany at the university in that city. De Candolle, fascinated by Moziño's drawings, which amounted to some fourteen hundred of plants and numerous others of animals, offered to work with him in classifying the new species. He believed Moziño's identifications to be of little value,[90] but offered, because the drawings were so precise, to undertake the task of identifying the known and classifying the new species of plants. In 1816 de Candolle asked Moziño to accompany him to Geneva where they could work together, but Moziño declined: "No, I am too old and sick; I am too unfortunate; take them [the manuscripts and drawings] to Geneva; I give them to you, and I entrust to your care my future glory."[91]

During the year following, Moziño attempted to secure readmittance to Spain, finally receiving permission in April, 1817. A cordial invitation to Madrid by the Spanish Minister of Marine Juan Jabat prompted him to ask de Candolle for the return of his drawings, with the exception of 305 duplicate originals. The Swiss botanist, not wanting to lose them completely, had a number of artists and amateurs of Geneva trace as many as possible "and in less than eight days 860 sketches were copied entirely and 119 preserved in the form of rough drafts."[92] Today this collection has assumed additional significance since most of the original drawings then in Moziño's possession have not come to light.

[90] As Rickett points out (*ibid.*, p. 78), Moziño undoubtedly made mistakes since he was limited to a few standard works, mostly those of Linnaeus, had no access to the herbaria upon which the works were based, and was attempting to classify a flora which was largely new to science.

[91] Alphonse Louis de Candolle, ed., *Memoires et souvenirs de Augustin-Pyramus de Candolle* (Geneva, 1862), p. 288.

[92] *Ibid.*, pp. 288–89. As a result of the drawings, now housed in the Conservatoire Botanique (Geneva), de Candolle and his colleagues identified 17 new genera and 271 new species which the Swiss botanist included in his *Systema* and *Prodomus* published during the 1830's. Two honoring Nootka are *Polygala nutkanus* and *Rubus nutkanus*. See also Alphonse L. de Candolle, ed., *Calques des dessins de la Flore du Mexique de Mociño et Sessé qui ont servi de types d'espèces dans le Systema ou le Prodomus* (Geneva, 1874).

There is no evidence that Moziño ever returned to Madrid. The author of *Noticias de Nutka* died in Barcelona, Spain, in May, 1820, as yet little recognized or appreciated in the country to which he had dedicated his life's work.[93]

[93] Rickett, "Royal Botanical Expedition to New Spain," p. 79. Moziño was buried on May 19, 1820, in the parochial church of St. James of Barcelona.

# NOTÍCIAS ÐE NUTKA

## AN ACCOUNT OF NOOTKA SOUND IN 1792

*Of Its Discovery, Location, and Natural Products;*
*About the Customs of Its Inhabitants, Government,*
*Rites, Chronology, Language, Music, Poetry,*
*Fishing, Hunting, and Fur Trade: With an Account*
*of the Voyages Made by Europeans, Particularly*
*Spaniards, and of the Agreement Made Between Them*
*and the English.*

*There is Added a Brief Dictionary of the*
*Nootkan Language, and the Entire Work is*
*Illustrated with Drawings.*

*By*
*D. Joseph Mariano Moziño Suárez de Figueroa, Botanist-*
*Naturalist of the Royal Expedition of New Spain*
*and also that of the Limits to the North of*
*California in the Year of 1793.*

# ARTICLE NO. I

*Concerning the discovery of Nootka or the Island of Mazarredo,[1] its location, climate, natural products in general; the size, physique, adornments, clothing, and weapons of its inhabitants*

ON THE eastern coast of the small island which today is known by the name of Mazarredo lies Nootka Sound. Although it was sighted by the Spanish pilot Don Juan Pérez in the year 1774,[2] [the sound] did not gain notoriety until 1778, when the indefatigable James Cook explored it and found there an abundance of furs, the trade in which he rightly presumed would be advantageous to his nation.[3]

The island [Nootka] is situated between 49°35′16″ and

[1] The island, which lies along the northwest coast of Vancouver Island, was called Mazarredo after José de Mazarredo (1745–1812), a famous Spanish admiral who commanded an expedition to the Philippines in 1777 and later distinguished himself against the British at Gibraltar. The manuscript in the Beinecke Collection of the Yale University Library, hereafter cited as the Yale MS, is titled "Relación de la Isla de Mazarredo."

[2] See "Diario de la Navegación hecha por el Alferez Graduado D. Juan Pérez de ord. del Sr. Bucareli a la altura de los 55 grados donde está situada la entrada y Bahía de su nombre en la fragata *Santiago*, alias la *N^a Galicia*, San Blas, 3 de Noviembre de 1774, MN, MS 335; AGN, Historia 62.

[3] Cook's expedition was in Nootka Sound from March 30 to April 26, 1778; see Cook, *A Voyage to the Pacific Ocean*, Vol. II, and Moziño, Article 8, pp. 64–68.

[ 3 ]

49°50′30″ north latitude and 110°4′ and 110°33′ longitude west of Tenerife.[4] It forms a kind of trapezium or irregular trapezoid, the longest side of which runs west-northwest from Isla de los Puercos [Hog Island] to Esperanza Inlet,[5] a distance of about twenty-three and one-half miles. The east side is fifteen miles, the north side about twenty-one miles, and the west side fifteen miles or five leagues.[6]

When seen from the sea, the island presents at first glance a most picturesque view, because its high mountains, always covered with pine and cedar, appear never to lose their verdancy. But upon going ashore one finds nothing anywhere except small sandy beaches, thickets, precipices, large sharp rocks, and huge craggy masses in disorderly array. Even volcanic lavas are found on the shores of a lake which lies at a distance of less than one-quarter of a mile from the anchorage.[7]

Some metallic veins surely run through these mountains, and

[4] This sentence is taken from the copy of the manuscript in the Revilla Gigedo Papers, Vol. XXX, Private Collection of Irving W. Robbins (hereafter cited as the Revilla Gigedo MS) and does not appear in the *Noticias de Nutka* published by Carreño. In the Yale MS it reads: "between 49° 35′ 16″ and —″north latitude and—to the West of Tenerife"; in the two copies of the manuscript in the Museo Naval in Madrid (MS 468 and MS 142), the sentence reads: "between 49° 35′ 16″ and 49° 50′ north latitude and 21° 21′ and 21° 51′ to the West of Tenerife [sic]." Bodega y Quadra, "Viaje de 1792" (AMAE, MS 145), gives a north latitude of 49° 29′ and a longitude of 21° 23′ west of San Blas.

[5] Called Hope Bay by Cook.

[6] The Revilla Gigedo MS gives the west side as "3 or 4 leagues," and the Yale MS "sixteen miles." Apparently the exact angle of closure was not determined, and the final size was merely an approximation.

[7] Anthropologist Philip Drucker, author of numerous ethnographic studies on the Indians of the Pacific Northwest, describes this coast in *The Northern and Central Nootkan Tribes* (Smithsonian Institution Bureau of American Ethnology Bulletin 144; Washington, D.C.: U.S. Government Printing Office, 1951), p. 8, as follows: "The woods, as seen from the water, seem to form an impenetrable mantle over the irregular surface of the land. . . . On shore the heavy rainfall supports a dense forest growth despite the poor soil (the bedrock is in most places barely covered by a thin layer of half-rotten leaves and needles, or moss, with but few shallow patches of soil)." See also A. J. Eardley, *Structural Geology of North America* (New York: Harper Brothers, 1951), pp. 455–59.

at least I think I am not deceiving myself in asserting that there are veins of copper, iron, lead, and perhaps some silver. This is something I could not verify because I lacked instruments, but I will perhaps report on it later when qualified persons have made an analysis of the rocks which I dug up and had sent for me to this capital [Mexico].[8]

If one can discuss the climate on the basis of the robust health which is enjoyed not only by all of us, but by all those we find here after two winters,[9] one can say that it is benign and incomparably better than that of the countries situated at the same parallel on the northeastern coast of America.[10] The long days of summer allow a sufficient amount of heat to be felt, and it is a rare year when frequent snows do not fall during the winter. The north wind generally blows at sunset; and the sea breeze from the northeast, which is always accompanied by calmness, comes at approximately nine in the morning. The north wind in the winter is extremely strong, and its duration almost continual. It roots out trees and puts any vessels which may be anchored in the port in great danger. During the rest of the year, the winds from the south and the southeast cause the most discomfort since they are accompanied by thick fogs and continuous rains which last at least forty-eight hours a week.[11] I have never heard thund-

[8] Alcalá Galiano and Valdés in "Relación del Viaje hecho por las Goletas Sutil y Mexicana," MN, MS 468, report that "the naturalist Don Francisco Mosiño asserts that there are some veins of metal in the mountainous terrain of this island . . . of iron and copper and one of silver."

[9] The Yale MS reads "the robust health enjoyed by the Spanish, English, and Boston-men after two winters. . . ."

[10] The New Englander John Hoskins (Howay, ed., *Voyages of the Columbia*," p. 280) does not agree: "The climate of this part of the country (if I may be permitted to judge) is certainly much milder though not so healthy as that on our side of the continent."

[11] Archibald Menzies gives a good description of this condition (Newcombe, ed., *Menzies' Journal*, p. 106): "In the evening [of August 26, 1792] we were abreast of the West entry into Nootka Sound but as it was hazy we stood off and on all night. . . . Next day . . . dark hazy weather & some drizzling rain that greatly retarded our progress & entirely obscured the inland mountains from our view. . . . In the morning of the 28th we stood again with a light favorable breeze from the Shore, but a thick fog still

er or seen lightning even on the days during which I experienced the worst storms. According to the accounts of the inhabitants, they have rarely seen these terrible phenomena, even in the most rigorous part of winter.

The topsoil has very little thickness. This can be recognized without the slightest difficulty because it began to be formed by the decomposition of mosses and other tender plants just a few centuries ago.[12] It is almost impossible for even the most resolute person to penetrate the interior [of the island], because it contains a multitude of deep gorges and the thick underbrush common to all forests. The natives inhabit only the beaches, and the mountains are reserved for the bears, lynxes, raccoons, weasels, squirrels, deer, and so forth.[13] I realized that birds were scarce because of the small number that I was able to arouse.[14] I was barely able to see a woodpecker, a hooked-bill sparrow, two hummingbirds, and two larks. The rest of the birds inhabit only the seashore, because it is their source of food, but even here the number of species is not abundant nor is the incidence great of the few species that do exist. There are white-headed falcon, yellow-speckled falcon, sparrow hawks, crows, herons, geese, seagulls, and so forth.[15]

---

hovering over the Land . . . we were obliged to stand off. . . ." According to Philip Drucker (personal communication, December 11, 1967), Friendly Cove is a poor anchorage. Not only northers but southeast storm winds (frequent through the winter) blow in there with heavy seas. They are the most dangerous on the west coast of Vancouver Island. Thunderstorms with lightning also occur in the area.

[12] Hoskins observed that "there is but little good soil which is on the low land and in the vallies and it is formed from decayed trees, rotten moss and leaves which are swept down from the mountains by the heavy torrents of rain . . . this is about two or three feet deep" (Howay, ed., *Voyages of the "Columbia,"* p. 280).

[13] John Ledyard listed "foxes, sables, hares, marmosets, ermines, weazles, bears, wolves, deer, moose, dogs, otters, beavers, and a species of weazle called the glutton" (Munford, ed., *Ledyard's Journal*, p. 70; see also Robert M. Storm's "Notes on Animals," pp. 243–45 therein).

[14] Cook agreed: "Birds in general are not only rare as to the different species, but very scarce as to numbers" (Synge, ed., *Cook's Voyages*, p. 432).

[15] In his "Catálogo de los Animales y Plantas," Moziño classifies forty

Our ships have carried a colony of rats to these uncivilized countries and these, having multiplied prodigiously, cause serious damage to the houses of our settlement. These houses are located on the best land included within the port area, at less than a crossbow's shot from the anchorage and next to the small cove in which the English Captain John Meares built his hut in the year 1787.[16] All that piece of land is converted into gardens, the produce of which has the most exquisite flavor, but all the diligence of Captain Pedro Alberni, who commanded the troops there, was useless in successfully cultivating the grains that constitute the basis of our sustenance.[17] Wheat and corn were always a failure; the latter grew vigorously and the former grew slowly, but I never saw either form heads of grain. Barley, on the contrary, gave some hope.

Possibly a new fertilization of these lands, debilitating its vegetative force a little in some parts and augmenting it in others, would provide nearly a mile of planted fields from the lagoon to the Maquinna River on a strip not less than thirty feet across at its narrowest. It is obvious that a successful harvest of a crop of

different birds according to the Linnaean system. See Plates 14, 15, and 16 for drawings of the marbled murrelet, California quail, and red crossbill. Bodega y Quadra ("Viaje de 1792") commented at Monterey: "One of the rarest and most beautiful birds is a quail which the naturalists have called Tetrao de California; one can see the drawing of it. Its meat is extremely tasty, and it is hunted in abundance."

[16] John Boit described the Spanish settlement at Nootka as containing "about 50 Houses indifferently built (except the Governors, which was rather *grand* than otherways). There was about 200 Inhabitants, consisting of Spaniards and Peru Indians, but no females. . . . There was two Botanists resided with Governor [Moziño and Maldonado]" (Howay, ed., *Voyages of the "Columbia,"* p. 410; Howay agrees with Joseph Ingraham's statement that "the village consists of 16 houses"). Menzies wrote: "After leaving the Governor's [house], we . . . found several other Houses erected here by the Spaniards as Barracks, Store House & an Hospital on the Scite of the Old Village formerly occupied by Maquinna the Chief . . ." (Newcombe, ed., *Menzies' Journal,* p. 111). See Plates 12 and 13 and map in Plate 2. Articles 8 and 11 herein concern John Meares.

[17] A more complete discussion of Alberni's efforts in 1790 is given in Article 10, pp. 77–80. The gardening at Nootka referred to was actually begun by Esteban José Martínez.

grain on such a plot would sustain a small garrison, which in turn could maintain this establishment. But how many trees would have to be rooted out? How many rocks would have to be removed? And how much tenacity would be necessary to clear out the roots and burn out the seeds of the many wild plants that occupy this terrain? Among them one finds many grasses, several brushwoods, andromedas, and berry bushes whose present luxuriance, it seems to me, does not forecast failure for the more useful plants that might be cultivated later.[18]

In regard to livestock, I believe that goats and pigs would prove successful here and would multiply within a very few years. The pasturage is very scarce for cattle and sheep, and if they should number more than one hundred head, it would not be easy to store a supply of dry leaves for the winter.

Fishing is abundant, and there are various edible varieties; many are of a delicate flavor like sole, salmon, cod, sardines, squid, and so forth.[19]

One finds springs of fresh water everywhere, and the lake of

---

[18] Bodega y Quadra was optimistic about cultivating the land: "My long stay in this port has enabled me to become acquainted with the advantages of the land in order to sustain a regular establishment. The soil is fertile, and the small portions of it that have been cultivated up to this time produce delightful gardens; the potatoes reach a considerable size, and these alone provide an article of subsistence in case of necessity. Along the west part there is an extension of nearly one mile which could be converted into wheat fields capable of providing bread for a thousand people . . . there is an esplanade which could be used for the planting of corn . . . [and] when these grains degenerate there remains a substantial recourse in the bulbous root of the Kamschatka Lily [see Article 2, p. 21, and Plate 22, herein], which grows wild throughout the entire island on the land that appears least useful, and this would serve as a savory bread, when it has been worked little, and would augment itself prodigiously later when new colonists cultivated it. Livestock would also prosper, especially goats and pigs; sufficient pasturage is lacking in the winter for cattle and sheep" (Bodega y Quadra, "Viaje de 1792").

[19] The names by which Moziño identified the various kinds of fish were often those common to European species or fish of Mexican waters (see Appendix B). The sardines of his list were undoubtedly a kind of smelt. See Plates 17 and 18 for drawings of *Cyprinus americanus?* and *Scomber? mahvinos*.

which I spoke a short while before has very pure and abundant water. It is not small in size and is usually more than ten fathoms deep.

Our residence of more than four months on that island enabled me to learn about the various customs of the natives, their religion, and their system of government.[20] I believe I am the first person who has been able to gather such information, and this was because I learned their language sufficiently to converse with them.[21]

The height of the common person is below average; that of the chiefs is medium; this difference may be due to the different occupations to which the former apply themselves from childhood. I was never able to observe a fat person among them, and even those we might call well built were very few.[22]

Their heads are elongated, not because of a natural defect but because from their birth they are placed in an oblong box which serves as a portable cradle.[23] In this they are held with strong

[20] The "natives" Moziño refers to were members of the Moachat confederacy inhabiting Nootka Sound; the term "Nootkan" today is a linguistic designation for members of the Wakashan stock extending from Cape Cook to Cape Flattery. See Drucker, *Northern and Central Nootkan Tribes*, pp. 5–6, 228–31. According to Meany (*Vancouver's Discovery of Puget Sound*, pp. 44–45), "The name by which these Indians know their village is 'Mowitch-at,' meaning 'people of the deer.' . . . The forests literally abound in deer. . . . It is not possible to trace the origin of all the words in the [Chinook] jargon but 'Mowitch' means 'deer,' and it is shown that this came from the Nootka Ianguage."

[21] The Yale MS reads: "The residence of more than four months of the members of the Botanical Expedition on that Island facilitated their learning about the various customs of the natives. I believe that they have been the first ones . . . to converse with them. We used these conversations to make the following report."

[22] Robert Haswell commented in March, 1789, that "the natives of the sound are below the middle size they indid are prity Large about the sholders and those parts of their body they keep in exercise are well proportioned thier principle employment being paddling their arms . . ." (Howay, ed., *Voyages of the "Columbia,"* p. 60); Ledyard reported that they were "rather above the middle stature, copper-coloured, and of an athletic make" (Munford, ed., *Ledyard's Journal*, p. 71).

[23] Drucker, *Northern and Central Nootkan Tribes*, p. 122, describes the process of artificial deformation of the child's head. See Plate 7.

bindings so that they always remain with this deformed con-figuration:[24] the forehead is raised up; the nose is flattened at the bridge and widened at the nostrils; the cheek-bones are raised and set wide apart, which makes the majority of them wide-faced; and almost all of them are round-faced. The size of their eyes is as variable as their natural expressions. A languid look is rather frequent among them, but rarely does one find a stupid-looking one. On the contrary, I noticed in many such a lively expression that, through it alone, one could guess many of their thoughts with little question. Their teeth are even and so strong that they retain them even at an advanced age. Perhaps the animal diet to which they are generally accustomed causes their teeth a loss of whiteness which, nevertheless, some of them always maintain.

Their necks are short and thick, and their backs proportionately wide. Rare is the person who does not have prominent ankles and the toes of his feet inclined toward the inside. This probably re-sults from the uncomfortable position in which they are seated when they travel in their canoes. All of this causes, therefore, an awkward method of walking which is especially noticeable in the women, who take slow steps.

Their hair is long, straight, and thick, varying in color from dark blond to chestnut and black. Their beard and body hair grows with the same regularity as in other men. Among the old men, the only ones who let it grow, it becomes as abundant and long as that of our Capuchins and Bethlehemites.[25] The young men pull it out hair by hair, either with their fingers or more often with tweezers which they make from small shells. The women, in the same manner, pull out the hair with which nature seems to have wanted to hide the sex organs.[26]

[24] The "Relación del Viaje hecho por las Goletas Sutil y Mexicana" re-ported that the natives were undoubtedly born with their heads ending in a point and this "should not be attributed to the fact that they are placed in oblong boxes which serve as beds or that their heads are molded with bind-ings."

[25] Spanish religious orders.

[26] Moziño calls these *"organos del pudor."*

9. "Sardine" fishing

10. *Interior view of Maquinna's house, in which the chief is shown dancing and his servants are singing and playing musical instruments*

11. *The coming-of-age celebration of Princess Izto-coti-clemot*

12. *View of Nootka Sound from the shore of the Spanish establishment*

13. *View of the establishment of Nootka; the letters AB designate the site occupied by Captain Meares*

14. Diomedea exulans? [Brachyramphus marmoratus], *marbled murrelet*

15. Tetrao californica [Lophortyx californica], *California quail*

16. Loxia curvirostra, *red crossbill*

The quantity of grease with which they adorn their bodies, and the red ochre with which they paint them, does not permit one to observe their natural color.[27] Because of this, I was forced to presume from the color of the children that they are not as dark as the Mexicans; and I was able to confirm this suspicion by the coincidence of finding the Princess Izto-coti-clemot very scrubbed on one of the ceremonial days when we all went with the commandant to congratulate her at her village. We saw a tender rose color in her face which tended toward being slightly pallid.

They are accustomed from childhood to pierce three or four holes through their ear lobes and one or two in the cartilage between their nostrils. The latter holes now have no other purpose except to hold some pins which they often thread through them, since they no longer use the nose rings to which they were accustomed when Captain Cook was there.[28] From their ears they hang various threads or bands, which they knot separately slightly more than one inch from the ear. From these they often hang some little doubled metal plates of copper in the form of a cylinder from an inch and a half to two inches in length. Others wear up to three and four earrings together, threaded with neither order nor proportion and with no attempt to make the adornment equal on both sides.

As a necklace around their throats, they string together various fishbones, spines of the Venus shell,[29] and frequently some glass

[27] Cook wrote: "Their colour we could never positively determine, as their bodies were incrusted with paint and dirt; though when these were well rubbed off, the whiteness of the skin appeared almost to equal that of Europeans" (Synge, ed., *Cook's Voyages*, p. 433).

[28] "In these holes [of the ears] they hang bits of bone, quills fixed upon a leathern thong, small shells, bunches of woollen tassels, or pieces of thin copper, which our beads could never supplant. The septum of the nose on many is also perforated and some wear . . . small, thin pieces of iron, brass or copper, shaped almost like a horse-shoe. . . . The rings of our brass buttons, which they eagerly purchased, were appropriated to this use" (Synge, ed., *Cook's Voyages*, p. 433).

[29] Moziño was undoubtedly confusing dentalium shells (see Drucker, *Northern and Central Nootkan Tribes*, pp. 100, 111–13) with the similar-

beads which have become available through trade with Europeans. They arrange their bracelets in the same way, and they like to wear similar strings on their ankles.

Hair styles vary somewhat; the common one consists of wearing the hair loose, cut evenly at the ends. Others wear it in the form of a simple braid, tied with a band to which are attached some cedar leaves in the form of a topknot. From the inner bark of this tree,[30] they remove some fibers which they pound [to shred] and afterward tint with a kind of red ochre. The cedar fibers are placed in the form of a circle around the head, making a crown. During fiesta days, they place down plucked from ducks, eagles, and herons over their hair, and use a whale grease, which they call *Ha-ca-miz*, as pomade.[31]

They rub their entire bodies with this pomade and then decorate themselves with some of it mixed with powdered red ochre. They apply it so evenly that it does not look artificial but like a natural color.[32] The luxury of savages throughout almost all the world, as Montesquieu observes, consists in the variety of colors with which they disfigure their faces. Our experience has been that this custom has not been frequent among these natives, but that they do observe it, nevertheless, during the days of some festivity. The extravagant taste of each one is what sets the rule

---

appearing spines of the Venus clam (*Pitar lupanaria*), which occurs along the west coast of Mexico.

[30] Both the red cedar (*Thuja plicata*) and yellow cedar (*Chamaecyparis nootkaensis*) were common sources of bark used in making various materials for basket and textile weaving. See Philip Drucker, *Indians of the Northwest Coast* (Garden City, N.Y.: The Natural History Press, 1963), pp. 61–64.

[31] "They have long black hair, which they generally wear in a club on the top of the head, they fill it when dressed with oil, paint and the downe of birds" (Munford, ed., *Ledyard's Journal*, p. 71).

[32] Cook apparently was not impressed. "But as they rub their bodies constantly over with a red paint, mixed with oil, their garments by this means contract a rancid, offensive smell and a greasy nastiness, so that they make a very wretched, dirty appearance" (Synge, ed., *Cook's Voyages*, p. 433).

in this area. I saw some faces colored blacker than an Ethiopian, others were red, others lead-colored, others white, and some of them mixed all the colors haphazardly, attempting to place different designs on each cheek. But what is noteworthy in this matter is that *taises* never paint around their eyes. Only the princes have the privilege of making unusual figures with the paint; the commoners[33] can only tint the entire face, including their eyelids and forehead, without any design.

Their dress is very simple. It commonly consists of a square cape woven from beaten cedar fibers and the wool of some quadruped, which I suspect to be a bison or mountain goat. They are provided with these by trade with the Nuchimanes,[34] who perhaps have some commerce with the tribes of the continent where these beasts are found in abundance.[35] The capes scarcely reach the ankles and even leave their bodies completely exposed along the entire right side; this is the shoulder on which they wear the strap that forms the opening for the head.[36]

This outfit is used more by custom, or perhaps for protection against the inclemencies of the cold, than for decency. Either because it is natural among them or because they have eliminated all sentiments of modesty entirely, the men frequently abandon

[33] Moziño uses the Spanish word *"plebeyo"* or *"plebe"* for commoner.
[34] Also spelled Muchimanes. These were most likely Nimpkish Kwakiutl. The southern Kwakiutl tribes occupied Quatsino Sound north of Cape Cook and the east coast of Vancouver Island to Cape Mudge. The Nootkan language is related to Kwakiutl, and they share many cultural traits. See Drucker, *Indians of the Northwest Coast*, p. 4.
[35] Probably mountain goat from Kwakiutl. Cook thought the wool came from different animals, "as the fox and brown lynx," although Ledyard observed that the Indians used the hair of dogs, "mostly white and of the domestic kind." Haswell described the garment as "composed of wool of the mountain sheep," whereas Vancouver and Menzies noted that the animal "from which the fine white wool comes" had small straight horns and was probably a goat. See Howay, *Voyages of the "Columbia,"* p. 60; Munford, ed., *Ledyard's Journal*, p. 71; Newcombe, ed., *Menzies' Journal*, p. 154; and F. W. Howay, "The Dog's Hair Blankets of the Coast Salish," *Washington Historical Quarterly*, IX (April, 1918), 83–92.
[36] See Plate 8.

this clothing and appear stark naked, without so much as covering their private parts with their hands, even though they might be in a group of numerous women. The women, on the contrary, preserve more decency. In addition to using the capes doubled, and drawing in the inner part with a narrow twisted cord, they hang a thin piece of cloth with a long fringe from the belt. This is made from the same cedar fibers used in weaving the capes. In a similar manner they usually have their breasts hidden under a short cape or closed cloak which is of the same material and made purposely in such a way that not a single seam is visible.[37] Their best clothing consists of the finest and most delicate material. They decorate all its edges with a border of otter skin and a plush or velvet material which they make by using the soft fur of the same animal as nap, and the fibers and wool already referred to for the weft and warp.

The men also dress in bearskins, which are extremely black, large, and have very long hair.

The sea otter provides a garment reserved only to the nobles of the first rank. It is formed from three good skins, two of which are left whole; from the third are made a number of equal strips, the ends of which protrude on both sides, and of this they make a cuff that has a certain elegance. The underside is ordinarily painted red with whimsical figures. When the weather is hot, they leave the fur on the outside; reversed, it provides them with great protection in winter. In order to augment their finery, they sew on various tails of the same amphibious animal as a kind of trimming placed on the suit.

We saw [chief] Maquinna with an excellent cape made of many skins of the finest sable [mink or marten?], joined together with such skill that much care was necessary to distinguish the seams on the reverse side, which were imperceptible on the fur side. This same chief sometimes appeared before us with another

[37] See Plate 6.

cape of rather exquisite weasel skins, in addition to one he also wore of deerskin, tanned with great softness.[38]

To protect themselves from the sun, they wear hats or caps of badger or raccoon skin. But more common are two kinds of hats woven over appropriate molds from tule or very flexible cattails joined with narrow strips taken from the ribs of a feather. This forms a white background on which the designs with which they are decorated stand out. These are always representations of the equipment used in fishing for whales. The shape of the hat is like a truncated cone, more or less elevated, upon which the nobles superimpose another small one that terminates in a sharp point. Those of the commoners are of a coarser material and have no designs; both affix their hats with chin stays or straps of any kind of cord.[39]

The profound peace which they enjoyed all the time we stayed with them did not give me the opportunity to observe a true war dress, but I was able to infer from a martial dance they gave for us that for fighting they use double, well-cured animal skins. Their dress differs from that [the leather jackets] of our soldiers of the *Provincias Internas* only by being longer and having evil figures painted on them. In these cases [of war dress], they hang from their waist a *tali* [strap], made from the same skin, which reaches almost to their knees. On this strap are found many strings, inserted in four or six parallel lines, to which are attached fish bones and quills of eagle feathers. They tie some deer hoofs in the ends, probably in order to intimidate the enemy with the noise these appendages make when the warrior is walking.[40]

[38] See Plate 5.

[39] Cook described their shape as "a truncated cone, or like a flowerpot, made of fine matting, having the top frequently ornamented with a round or pointed knob" with a chinstrap "to prevent its blowing off" (Synge, ed., *Cook's Voyages*, p. 433). See Charles C. Willoughby, "Hats from the Nootka Sound Region," *American Naturalist*, XXXVII (1903), 65–68.

[40] Ledyard noted that they had "also a kind of armor that covers the body from the breast downward to the knees; this consists of moose-skin,

[15]

Maquinna today is provided with a handsome helmet and coat of mail of tin plate worked in scales which our [Spanish] Commandant [Juan Francisco de la Bodega y Quadra] gave to him.[41]

Their only weapons are the lance and arrows; the shaft of the lance is almost five yards long, and the barb more than one *geme* (the longest distance from the end of the thumb to the tip of the forefinger); the former is of pine or cedar, and the latter of copper, shell, or iron. Their bows are small and not very flexible, and their arrows very poorly prepared; they are suspended from the shoulder over the back in a quiver of bearskin.[42] Today they handle all the European arms of flints, sabers, and swords with special dexterity. Despite the fact that these [weapons] are an article of commerce for which many of them have singular affection, in time the exchange of arms may be fatal to the very ones who have provided them. The English captains Brown and Baker have already experienced in Clayoquot the fatal consequences of two hundred guns, and I do not know how many barrels of powder, which were supplied to Wickinanish.[43]

---

covered externally with slips of wood sewed to the leather transversely . . ." (Munford, ed., *Ledyard's Journal*, p. 76).

[41] Moziño says only "which our Commandant gave to him," whereas the Yale MS includes Bodega y Quadra's name.

[42] "These people are possessed of a variety of impliments calculated for war, hunting, fishing and other purposes . . . remarkably analogous to ancient models, particularly the lance. . . . They have also good bows and arrows, and stone hatchets" (Munford, ed., *Ledyard's Journal*, p. 76).

[43] According to Peter Puget, Vancouver received a complaint from Captain James Magee of the Boston ship *Margaret* that Captains William Brown of the *Butterworth* and James Baker of the *Jenny* had fired upon the Indians in Clayoquot Sound a few weeks before (August, 1792) and should be charged with piracy (Anderson, *Life and Voyages of George Vancouver*, p. 111). Apparently the crew of the *Butterworth* had tried to rob the Indians of their furs and, encountering resistance, fired upon them and killed four. The natives retaliated, killing one sailor and wounding several others. See F. W. Howay, "The Voyage of the Hope: 1790–1792," *Washington Historical Quarterly*, XI (January, 1920), 25–26.

# ARTICLE NO. 2

*Description of their houses, furniture, and utensils; of their food and drink*

THE appearance of their houses indicates misery, disorder, abandonment, and filth everywhere. In order to construct them, they place some thick pine trunks vertically in the ground with notches upward. Upon these is placed an enormous round beam of the same wood, which, resting horizontally, serves as the base for the roof. The supports in the middle are higher so that the roof is pitched toward the sides; the walls are composed of planks of extraordinary size placed parallel and on edge overlapping each other and fastened to the supports with cords made from the bark of the same tree [pine] or from the cedar [withes].[1] Some squared holes are often made [in the walls], and some small sticks nailed to the upper part of these serve as curtains. Maquinna has inserted glass panes in there and thereby formed windows.[2]

At the beginning [of construction], the doorway is left open at the place where the planks of the wall best permit, and I be-

[1] It is possible that Moziño's "pine" was red cedar and the withes of yellow cedar. See Drucker, *Northern and Central Nootkan Tribes*, pp. 68–70, for an excellent description and illustration of a Nootkan house frame.

[2] The glass panes were a gift to Maquinna from Bodega y Quadra. See Article 7, p. 56.

[ 17 ]

lieve that it is never closed except with some mat cut to its size. The roof is covered with planks, similar to those which they have used underneath, and these are neither fastened nor tied to the beams which sustain them. They remain movable so that they can be separated from each other when the inhabitants want to receive more light or allow smoke to escape. The only thing they take care about is to see that the edges of each upper plank rest exactly over the two underneath, in the same manner as we use roof tiles in order to protect the interior of the house from the rain.

The intermediate beam is supported by some thick, cylindrical columns of the same pine, on which are sculptured human faces deformed by the size and grotesqueness of their features. These are given the name of *Tlama*.[3] The first travelers assumed that these figures were objects of superstitious worship, and I also suspected the same until informed otherwise by the Indians themselves.[4] I learned that they were nothing more than a simple decoration, and if by chance a figure had some significance, it was purely that given to it by the man whose labor had brought the [sculptured] tree to the place in which it was found.

Around the inside of the house are placed, some on top of others, a multitude of boxes of various sizes and commonly of one piece. Their lids consist of a plank that runs along two open grooves on the upper and inside parts. When the boxes are composed of various pieces, they are very firmly fitted together, and each piece is interlocked with the others in the same manner as those of our carpenters. The exterior is often decorated with

[3] See Plate 10.

[4] Cook (*A Voyage to the Pacific Ocean*, II, 317) noted that the general name of these images was "Klumma" and thought they were representatives of their gods or symbols of some religious or superstitious object, but also "had proofs of the little estimation they were held in. . . ." According to Drucker (*Northern and Central Nootkan Tribes*, p. 69), these "were not idols in the usual sense, but were special 'privileges' said to have been bestowed on a lineage ancestor by supernatural beings for use by him and his direct descendants."

[ 18 ]

molding inlaid with the teeth of different animals. Here they keep their capes, their masks, and, in general, all the belongings they consider worthwhile.

There are also, here and there, various platforms of mats which are used for beds. Each of them is in a compartment separated from the adjoining one by a small partition of panels which are scarcely more than a yard in height. From the beams are hung many strings of sardines and various other fish and shellfish used for the sustenance of the natives. On the walls are hung numerous bladders of various sizes, all filled with whale oil. In the best place in the house is found an oblong box a little more than two yards in length and half that in width. On the inside is painted a monstrous figure with a human face, but extremely ugly, with very long arms, claws like an eagle's, and feet like those of a bear. It is used for religious purposes to which I will refer later.[5]

Inside this same room of their house they make large fires, clean their fish, and remove shellfish and snails from their shells, leaving a large part of the remains thrown on the floor where it rots. This causes an unbearable repugnance to anyone who has not grown up in the midst of so much stench. The filth is incomparably greater in the houses of the *meschimes* [commoners], both because they are all generally found to be sordid and also because the women do not show the least vestige of what we call cleanliness.[6] I saw them many times defleaing themselves among each other and eating as many fleas as they could find.

The kitchen furniture is all of wood, and they have very few utensils. Some buckets serve as jars, and some small painted trays are used as plates. The giant abalone shell, which is brought from Monterey and New Holland [Australia], is the most luxurious container with which they are acquainted. They light a fire by

[5] See Article 5, p. 39.
[6] Moziño uses the Nootkan word *meschimes* for commoners throughout. Cook thought all their houses were "filthy as hog-sties; everything in and about them stinking of filth, train-oil, and smoke" (*A Voyage to the Pacific Ocean*, II, 317).

[ 19 ]

rubbing two sticks together, and when this has made a blaze they put many stones in it to heat. These are taken out with a long pair of wooden tongs and cooled off inside the buckets in which the fish are soaking, until, by repeating this method, the fish are boiled. They also prepare them by roasting, either turning them over in the hot embers or running them through with a wooden spit.[7]

They obtain their principal sustenance from the sea, and they make abundant provisions for the months when fish are scarce by smoking fish to preserve them. Salt is entirely lacking, but I noticed another condiment (if one could call it that), which is whale oil, or that of sardines, which they mix according to their taste in their dishes of roasted or boiled foods. They also use deer meat, and I presume they scorn that of the bear and sea otter. They like geese and seagulls and other aquatic birds, but I have not been able to learn whether they use eagles for the same purpose, or whether they hunt them only to use their feathers.[8]

Upon asking Prince Hauitl the number of dishes Maquinna was accustomed to give the other *taises* when they came to visit him, I counted up to thirty-six, a number I judge comes from the several kinds of fish, birds, and animals on which they ordinarily subsist. Also, they do not fail to eat the vegetables that grow wild during the summer. For them the juicy berries of the andromeda are the most delicate fruit. They also consume with pleasure the three species of blackberries that grow among their forests; the vaccinium [huckleberry or blueberry], crabapples and wild pears, madrone berries, currants, and strawberries. The flowers and fruit

[7] Drucker, *Northern and Central Nootkan Tribes*, p. 62, supports this description: "The boiling of foods, done in wooden boxes with hot stones taken from the fire with tongs, was a simple process, whether dried dog salmon heads or partly filleted whole sockeye were the dish being prepared . . ."; on the other hand, Drucker reports that roasting in coals was used only slightly and that "piping hot food was not liked."

[8] Drucker, *ibid.*, p. 59, says that "eagles were caught in a number of ways for their feathers, and the flesh was not disdained as food in the fall when the birds were fat from eating salmon."

of the wild rose haw, the silver weed, the tender stalks of the angelica, the leaves of the lithosperm, the roots of the trailing clover, and the scaly onionlike bulb of the Kamchatka lily[9] are the vegetables which providence appears to have provided them in order to correct the alkaline imbalance caused by the continuous use of fish and seafood toward which these islanders are inclined.[10] I doubt that they like garlic because, even though they came in their canoes to sell it, it annoyed them greatly to see it on our tables.

They do not have any fermented beverage, and until they began to deal with Europeans they satisfied their thirst with nothing more than water. Since that time they have acquired quite an affection for wine, brandy, and beer, all of which they use excessively whenever there is someone who furnishes them liberally, but up until now the thought of procuring these liquors by means of commerce does not seem to have occurred to them.

Our contact has introduced bread to them, and they have demonstrated particular liking for it. Also as a result of this contact they have chocolate, sugar, brown sugar, and all the confections. They like coffee and tea excessively, but milk, butter, cheese, olive oil and vinegar, and all the spices that we ordinarily use cause them inexplicable annoyance. Now they are overcoming to a great degree the repugnance which our foods have caused them. They have become accustomed to soup, as long as it is

[9] Menzies (September 4, 1792) observed a number of Nootkan women digging in a meadow in "search of a small creeping root about the size of a pack thread. This I found to be the Roots of a new species of Trifolium [fimbriatum (wild clover)] which they always dig up at this time of the year for food. . . . Wherever this Trifolium abound the ground is regularly turned over in quest of its roots every year, though till this moment we ascribed such digging to their searching after the Sarane or Roots of *Lilium Camschatcensa* which we knew they collect & use as food here . . ." (Newcombe, ed., *Menzies' Journal*, p. 116–17); see Plate 22.

[10] See also Elmer Drew Merrill, *The Botany of Cook's Voyages* (Chronica Botanica, Vol. XIV; Waltham, Mass.: Chronica Botanica Co., 1954); and Helen M. Gilkey's "Notes on Plants" in Munford, ed., *Ledyard's Journal*, pp. 239–41.

not of vermicelli, noodles, and so forth; to cooked vegetables, excluding only cabbage; to roasts of mutton, beef, or deer, but not to chicken; and to salads of lettuce or broccoli only. Beans for them are the most delicious dish; they call them *Tais-frijoles*, which is to say "dish of the Kings." There was someone who wanted to indicate the great appreciation which this legume merited by not permitting it to be known in the future by any name other than *frijoles* [beans].

From the consistent reports that the Spaniards and Boston men have given us, it appears to be proved in an uncontestable manner that these savages have been cannibals.[11] In fact, they came on board the packet boat *San Carlos*, commanded by Lieutenant Don Salvador Fidalgo, with the cooked hand of a child, and took other limbs prepared in the same manner to other vessels. Certainly the abhorrence which they immediately perceived on our part, and the threats of punishment which they were promised for such execrable cruelty, have made them remove this viand from their tables; or, better yet, the precious peace which they have enjoyed has not permitted them to be supplied with prisoners, the unfortunate victims who became entombed in their stom-

[11] Esteban José Martínez, head of the Spanish expedition to Nootka in 1789, recorded in his diary on September 30, 1789, that "the chiefs are accustomed, when there is a scarcity of fish, to eat the boys whom they take as prisoners. Macuina, the principal chief of this village, and Keleken, have been the most addicted to this use of human flesh. However, it seems they are not in the habit of doing it now, because of the many protests by foreigners" (Martínez, *Diario*). Ledyard described the offering of "a human arm roasted" the taste of which "was very odious" and proceeded to give a short treatise on the "ancient custom of sacrificing human flesh" (Munford, ed., *Ledyard's Journal*, pp. 73–76). Haswell wrote in March, 1789: "Thes people are canables and eat the flesh of their vanqu[i]shed enemies and frequently of their slaves who they kill in Cool blud they make but little serimoney in owning the fact and I have seen them eat human flesh myself"; but Howay (*Voyages of the "Columbia,"* p. 66) notes: "The established opinion today is that the Indians of the Northwest Coast were not cannibals; and that anything that appeared to be cannibalism was in reality merely formal and a part of some ceremonial. Cook, Ledyard, Meares, Galiano and Valdés, Malaspina, Roquefeuil, and many others entertained the view that these people were cannibals; but not one well authenticated instance of cannibalism has been produced."

achs. Hauitl assured me that not everyone had eaten human flesh, nor did they all the time, just the fiercest warriors when they prepared to go to war. I doubt the truth of this story, because this wise Indian knew very well how much we detested this custom, and now that he could not contradict what so many honest men had said, he wanted at least to diminish the gravity and circumstances of a crime that makes even nature shudder.

# ARTICLE NO. 3

*System of government of the* tais, *or sovereign and high priest; about religious beliefs, their worship and superstitions; their funeral rites*

THE government of these people can strictly be called patriarchal, because the chief of the nation carries out the duties of father of the families, of king, and high priest at the same time. These three offices are so closely intertwined that they mutually sustain each other, and all together support the sovereign authority of the *taises*.[1] The vassals receive their sustenance from the hands of the monarch, or from the governor who represents him in the distant villages under his rule. The vassals believe that they owe this sustenance to the intercession of the sovereign with God. Thus the fusion of political rights with religious rights forms the basis of a system which at first glance appears more despotic than that of the caliphs and is so in certain respects, but which shows moderation in others. There is no intermediate hierarchy between princes and commoners. This latter condition includes all those who are not brothers or immediate relatives of the *tais*, and they are known by the name of *meschimes*. The

[1] The Spanish recorded the Nootkan word for "chief" as *tais*, Meares as *tighee*, and Cook, Vancouver, and others as *tyee*. This is considered the source for *tyee* as "chief" in Chinook jargon. See Meany, *Vancouver's Discovery of Puget Sound*, p. 45.

former are called *taiscatlati,* that is to say, brothers of the chief.[2]

The moderation of this system consists in the fact that the monarch, in spite of being convinced of the value of his orations, does not fail to recognize that these would be unfruitful for the sustenance of himself and his subjects if they did not also employ their working efforts in fishing, hunting, lumbering, and so forth. This obliges him to arm them like sons to defend themselves from their enemies at all risk, and to alleviate as much as possible the hardships of life. It would be very boring to express in detail the deeds that substantiate what I have referred to; suffice it to say that in Maquinna I have always observed inexpressible feeling over the loss of one of his subjects by death or flight; that his subjects treat him with familiarity but maintain at the same time an inviolable respect.

The *tais* always travels in the company of two or three princes of his blood and occupies the center of the canoe. At the two ends paddle the *meschimes,* and no one sits at his side except his relatives and his wives. When the chief retires, his men run hurriedly to accompany him, even if they are enjoying themselves, unless he himself occupies them with some other thing, or wishes to walk alone. The *tais* never works, and even to watch over those who assist in the fishing, he ordinarily assigns one of the *catlati.* He is the first minister of sacrifices, and the principal repository of the religious secrets.

I find it extremely difficult to give this religion an adequate name, unless I may call it a kind of Manicheism, because the

[2] The Nootkans placed considerable emphasis upon hereditary class distinctions. The chiefs constituted a true nobility and were set apart, purely by accident of birth, from the commoners. The principal chiefs of the district were those who owned the most property, the lower chiefs owned less, and the commoners owned nothing at all. The roles of each class were clearly defined, not only on formal occasions, but in everyday activities. Among the aristocracy (brothers or relatives of the chief) rank was based on primogeniture, and the descendants of younger sons formed a kind of middle class. Chiefs were expected to marry women whose fathers were of the same social status. Rank and privileges are discussed by Drucker, *Northern and Central Nootkan Tribes,* pp. 243–45.

[ 25 ]

natives recognize the existence of a God Creator, Preserver of all things.[3] They also believe in another malign deity, author of wars, of infirmities, and of death. They hate and detest this abominable originator of their calamities, while they venerate and exalt the benevolent God who created them. In his observance, the barbaric high priest fasts many days. He constantly abstains from the pleasures of love all the time that the moon is not full. He sings hymns accompanied by his family, honoring the benefactions of *Qua-utz* (which is what they call the Creator), and in sacrifice the *tais* throws whale oil into the flames and scatters feathers to the wind.[4]

The manner in which they relate the creation of man in the beginning is rather amusing. They say that God created a woman who was left perfectly alone in the obscure forests of Yuquatl,[5] in which lived deer without antlers, dogs without tails, and ducks without wings; that, isolated there, she cried day and night in her loneliness without finding the least means of remedying her sad situation until Qua-utz, sympathizing with her tears, allowed her to see on the ocean a very resplendent canoe of copper in which, with paddles of the same metal, many handsome young men

[3] Bodega y Quadra supported Moziño's opinion and, after having been in all of their houses, commented: . . . in none of them did I see true idols, because the large figures on the columns and some of the others are mere whims. When they are more hieroglyphic, they signify one of the most outstanding virtues of the chief. From all this, I cannot be persuaded that they ignore the existence of God, as some have suspected, because they recognize a Creator to whose goodness they owe their preservation . . ." ("Viaje de 1792").

[4] John Jewitt indicated that the natives believed in the existence of a Supreme Being and described a seven-day celebration in honor of this god, "Quahootze," "to return him their thanks for the past, and implore him future favors" (Robert Brown, ed., *The Adventures and Sufferings of John Jewitt . . . during a captivity of nearly three years among the Indians of Nootka Sound* (London: C. Wilson, 1896), pp. 116, 216); but Drucker notes that modern Nootkans believe in not one but four deities (Above Chief, Horizon Chief, Land Chief, and Undersea Chief) and have no knowledge of a single overall god (*Northern and Central Nootkan Tribes*, p. 152).

[5] Yuquatl (Yuqwot) was the Nootkan name for the site where the Spanish were located on the island of Nootka.

came paddling. Astonished by this spectacle, the island girl remained stunned at the foot of the tree, until one of the paddlers advised her that it was the All-Powerful who had had the goodness to visit that beach and supply her with the company she longed for. At these words the melancholy solitary girl redoubled her weeping; her nose began to run, and she sneezed its loathsome discharge onto the nearby sand. Qua-utz then ordered her to pick up what she had sneezed out, and to her astonishment she found palpitating the tiny body of a man which had just been formed.[6] She gathered it up, by order of the Deity, in a shell appropriate to its size, and was admonished to continue keeping it in other larger shells as it grew in size. After this, the Creator got into the boat again, after having allowed even the animals to share in his liberality, because at the same moment the deer saw antlers grow over his forehead, the dog began to wag a tail—with which he found himself provided—from one side to the other, and the birds were able to lift themselves by the wind and try out for the first time the gift of wings which they had just received. The man grew little by little, passing successively from one cradle to another until he began to walk. Having left his childhood, the first proof he gave of his early manhood was to impregnate his mistress, whose first-born created the family tree of the *taises* while the other siblings formed that of the common people.

I do not know what to say about Matlox, inhabitant of the mountainous district, of whom all have an unbelievable terror.[7] They imagine his body as very monstrous, all covered with stiff black bristles; a head similar to a human one, but with much greater, sharper, and stronger fangs than those of the bear; ex-

---

[6] Drucker (*Northern and Central Nootkan Tribes*, pp. 144 and 452) refers to Snot-Boy (*antōkt*) as the Transformer-Culture Hero in the myths of the northern and central Nootkan groups above Barkley Sound.

[7] Robert Haswell wrote in 1789 that the Indians had "several strange stories of this strange monster[.] they say they were doing some bad thing on the beach in some past ages when the dredfull fellow made his appearance . . ." (Howay, ed., *Voyages of the "Columbia,"* p. 64).

tremely long arms; and toes and fingers armed with long curved claws. His shouts alone (they say) force those who hear them to the ground, and any unfortunate body he slaps is broken into a thousand pieces. I presume that the story of Matlox has the same foundation as that of the creation of man, to which I have just referred; or that from most ancient times the tribe to which these natives owe their origin received some account of the existence of demons.[8]

They believe that the soul is incorporeal, and that after death it has to pass to an eternal life, but with this difference: the souls of the *taises* and their closest relatives go to join those of their ancestors in glory where Qua-utz resides. The commoners, or *meschimes*, have a different destiny; for them there awaits a Hell, called *Pin-pu-la*, whose prince is Iz-mi-tz. The former [souls of the *taises*] are the authors of the lightning and the rain; the lightning is testimony of their indignation and the rain of their feelings. Whenever any *tais* overcomes some calamity by his own efforts, the rains are the tears which his sympathetic ancestors spill from heaven; the lightning strikes when they discharge their arms to punish evil-doers. Those *taises* who abandon themselves to lust, the gluttons, the negligent in offering sacrifices, and the ones lazy in praying, suffer the miserable fate of a commoner at the end of their lives.

The difference existing between commoners and princes influences the distinction observed in their burial rites. The bodies of the *taises* and other princes are wrapped in exquisite otter skins, placed in a wooden chest, and suspended from some pine tree branch in the mountains. Every day four or six domestic servants [of the deceased] go to inspect it and are obliged to sing

---

[8] Modern writers list a number of demons or supernatural beings that plagued the lives of the Nootkan Indians. These included the Thunderbird, a huge man living in the remote snow-covered peaks, headless birds, and a mountain lion that walked backward and killed men with a long lance-like tail; even the "souls of Trees" were malignant ( Drucker, *Northern and Central Nootkan Tribes*, p. 153).

various funeral hymns around the tree; these are still heard by the soul, which does not abandon the locality of the body it once animated until the body is entirely destroyed. The *meschimes* are buried in the earth in order to be nearer the location of *Pin-pu-la*. There they do not have to worry about suffering, except that they consider it as suffering to be separated forever from their old masters, and to be incapable of ever elevating themselves to the high state in which these masters live. The *taises* do not believe this retribution unjust, which appears to be more the predestined compensation for the sheer accident of birth than for the personal merit of those individuals. They are convinced that since the commoners are able to enjoy the pleasures of sensuality at all times, not being subject to the painful observance of the fast, nor to the hard work of prayers (in all of which the chiefs are heavily obligated), they are not worthy of a reward which would liken them in a certain manner to the Deity.[9]

I could not ascertain the significance of a ridiculous ceremony which I observed the last time that I was in one of their villages. An old lady was found extended over a platform feigning death and another seated at her side was making melancholy cries. Quatlazape, Maquinna's brother, did not permit me to remain there, and taking me by the arm told me only that this was done for a dead person, and that at the end of two months they would conclude the dreary pageantry. They mourn the death of a *tais* four months, and all signs of mourning are confined to the cutting of the women's hair to a length of four or six fingers below the ears.

The belief that the monarch who presently governs them will in time become one of the fortunate ones, capable of overthrowing all the harmony of the elements at his pleasure, obliges the subjects to show him as much veneration as they consider appro-

[9] Jewitt described the funeral rites of Chief Tutusi (Tootoosch), who died in June, 1805, but expressed the opinion that Maquinna had no belief in life after death (Brown, ed., *Adventures of John Jewitt*, pp. 181, 217); Brown notes that Jewitt's statement is extremely suspect.

priate to a sacred person. Not even by accident is one permitted to lay his hands on the sovereign. One time, to demonstrate the close relationship which the commander of the frigate *Santa Gertrudis*[10] had with Maquinna, the officer threw some small stones at the Indian. The most ancient and distinguished of the nobles that were present held back his hand: with a *tais* (he told him) one does not play in this manner. Despite such extreme veneration, the *meschimes* present themselves in any manner in front of the chief, seating themselves indiscriminately, reclining, knocking each other down in his presence, and behaving in a manner that does not appear to preserve the marks of submission; except that they do not do this at his side, and promptly obey whatever orders he gives them, leaving their meal the instant that he orders them to do something.

---

[10] Alonzo de Torres.

# ARTICLE NO. 4

*Concerning the dignity of the* tais *and his marriages; fertility of the women; ceremonies with which they celebrate childbirths; accounts of other strange customs*

T HE dignity of the *tais* is hereditary from fathers to sons, and it passes regularly to the latter provided they are capable of governing, and provided the former feel themselves to be advanced in age. There were three principal *taises* whom we knew in Nootka, the superior of all in many respects being Maquinna, whose father died after the year 1778 in a war against the Tlaumases. I have not been able to determine in what area this nation resides, and the etymology indicates only that they are from the other part of the sea, without expressing the direction. His son and successor [Maquinna] avenged his death; going in person to the enemy villages, he took them by surprise and carried out a frightful massacre. Quio-comasia and Tlu-pana-nutl are the other two *taises*.[1] Their fathers still live, having re-

---

[1] The tribal organization of the Moachat confederacy provided for a principal chief (Maquinna) and a number of lesser chiefs whose relative rank, based upon ownership of property, was generally fixed. Moachat headquarters were at Friendly Cove (Yuquatl), and the tribe occupied sites at Copti, Tasis, and elsewhere in Nootka Sound. An originally independent group lived at the Tlupana Arm, but after they were given summer lodgings at Yuquatl these Indians eventually joined the Moachat confederacy. Tlu-pana-nutl was probably a chief of this group. Naturalist Archibald

tained at the time of their renunciation only the dignity of priest-hood, either because they believed it to be inalienable or because, with age, their superstition increased.

The brothers of the *tais* make up the second order of nobility, but this begins to be lost after two or three generations because the relatives who pass into the third degree do not participate. These fall rapidly into the class of *meschimes*, or commoners, which is the lowest of the state. The women share the status of their fathers and husbands.[2]

Polygamy is established among the *taises* and princes, or *catlati* [brothers of the *tais*], who consider it a sign of greatness to buy and maintain various wives.[3] I always noticed that one among them was constantly more privileged, and that even the other wives treated her with so much consideration that next to her they appeared as mere concubines. Their acquisition is very costly to the *taises*, who can obtain them from the hands of their fathers only at the cost of many sheets of copper, otter skins, shells, cloth of cedar bark, canoes, fish, and so forth, so that the person who has four or six daughters of normal appearance can count them as so many jewels whose price will make him ex-tremely rich. The *meschimes* almost always find themselves in-capable of incurring these expenses, because not being the own-ers of the fruits of their labor, except in a very small part, they can never collect the dowry. Thus, many of them die without be-ing married, and the few that have better luck must content themselves with just one wife, which they receive at the hands of

Menzies wrote that the British (in 1792) "were likewise visited by another aged Chief named *Floopannanoo* [Moziño's Tlu-pana-nutl], whose Tribe occupied one of the North west branches of the Sound & who Joined to a Countenance truly Savage, a most amiable & friendly disposition. . . . Both he & Hannapa seemed to be dependents of Maquinna . . ." (Newcombe, ed., *Menzies' Journal*, p. 115).

[2] Contrary to Moziño's statement, Drucker (*Northern and Central Noot-kan Tribes*, pp. 243–45) indicates that a woman retained the status of her father, rather than assuming that of her husband.

[3] The practice of polygamy, common among the Northwest Coast Indians, was mentioned by almost all the early European and American visitors.

their prince as a reward for their services. I do not know what the nuptial ceremonies are because not a single wedding was celebrated during our residence in that country.[4]

I deduce that the women are normally fertile, and assume that their period of fertility is more or less the same as that of Europeans, since I always saw small children and there were some pregnant women whose age did not seem to be under forty years. I do not know if they are helped by midwives during the time they give birth, but they certainly lack the difficult pregnancies to which our women are exposed. As soon as they throw off the afterbirth, they run into the sea and swim with great resolution.[5] What is strange is that after a son is born, if his father is a *tais*, he has to enclose himself in his lodge, seeing neither the sun nor the waves. He is fearful of gravely offending Qua-utz, who would leave both him and his son without life in punishment of his sin.

When the prince is more than one month old, there is a convocation of all the nobles and they give him his first name. His allegorical christening is performed either by the father himself or by another responsible person who is commissioned to do this. The new name is celebrated with banquets, songs, and dances, during each of which the prolific *tais* gives presents of otters, copper, shells, and as many precious items as he can afford to the nobles who have come to offer their congratulations.

Names are changed according to one's age, and in this matter

[4] Alcalá Galiano reported that the marriage ceremonies of the Nootkans consisted simply of entertainment supplied by friends of the newly married couple's families ("Relación del Viaje hecho por las Goletas Sutil y Mexicana"). Marriage among the Nootkans was considered a formal alliance between two family groups and was approved by a series of gift exchanges.

[5] Drucker suggests that "statements of even such good observers as Sproat [1868] and Moziño to the effect that women went about their daily affairs immediately after parturition are to be discounted; such women as they saw going about soon after child-bearing must have just been released from the confinement hut after the locally proper period of seclusion" (*Northern and Central Nootkan Tribes*, p. 119). Alcalá Galiano noted that the Indian women of Monterey, California, were also extremely hardy and returned to work in the field soon after giving birth ("Relación del Viaje hecho por las Goletas Sutil y Mexicana").

each new one of these is solemnized with greater luxury and magnificence than the first one. The discreet youth commended by Mr. Meares under the name of Quia-sechiconuc was called Tlu-pa-nia-pa in his infancy, Na-na-fa-mitz in his childhood, Gu-gu-me-ta-tzautlz in his puberty, the name I have given above in his youth, and now, finally, Quio-comasia, having received the privileges of manhood, at which time he entered into the dignity of *tais*. His final name means "excessively liberal prince." That of his father, Ana-pe-tais, means "outstanding among the others," like a great pine among small ones; that of Maquinna, "Tais of the Sun."

As soon as the menstrual flow appears in a girl for the first time, they celebrate in the same manner, and her name is also changed. If by chance she is the daughter of the principal chief of the *taises*, this proclamation occurs on the same day. We were present to congratulate Maquinna for that of his daughter Izto-coti-clemot,[6] who before this time was called Apenas.[7]

The savage pomp with which they solemnize this function is worthy of note.[8] At one of the corners of the house which is situated at the edge of the forested Copti Mountains, they set up a platform, held up by four thick props in the form of columns, on the same level as the roof.[9] On top they constructed a kind of balcony, entirely enclosed by planks. Both this and the columns were painted white, yellow, red, blue, and black, with various large figures of poor design. They were also decorated with mirrors of various sizes; and two busts, with arms open and hands

[6] Also spelled Iztocoti-tlemoc, Istocoti-tlemoc, and Istocoti-clemot.
[7] See Edward Sapir, "A Girl's Puberty Ceremony among the Nootka Indians," *Transactions of the Royal Society of Canada*, Ser. 3, VII (1913), 67–80.
[8] Menzies reported that the daughter of Maquinna "was a young Girl about thirteen years of age named Apinnas, who the Spaniards informed us had been lately recognized & inaugurated in a most pompous & solemn manner by the whole Tribe as the Successor of her Father" (Newcombe, ed., *Menzies' Journal*, p. 117).
[9] See Plate 11.

extended, were placed in the corners to signify the magnificence of the monarch. At the foot of the columns was a leveled ring in the form of an arena surrounded by a wooden fence.

Inside the house on some new mats was the young princess, dressed in the finest materials of cedar bark and attired with innumerable necklaces of small pointed pieces of some species of Venus shell [dentalium shells]. Cut all the same, these have a beautiful luster and the shape of glass beads. Her hair was parted in the middle and divided into two equal parts, fastened tightly at the ends by means of many cylinders of well-polished copper, similar to those hanging from her ears. Their weight could not have been less than one Castilian pound.

Maquinna took his daughter by the hand, conducted her to the balcony, placed her in its center, and remained at her right; at the left was his brother Quatlazape. The assembly of numerous natives occupying the leveled arena and beach became profoundly silent. The chief directed his voice to all: "My daughter Apenas (he told them) is no longer a girl, but a woman: from this time forth she will be known by the name Izto-coti-clemot; that is, the great Taisa of Yuquatl." All responded with a shout: "Hua-cás, Hua-cás, Maquinna, Hua-cás-Izto-coti-clemot"; an expression which equals our *viva*, since the greatest eulogy among these people is always demonstrated by the friendship which the word *Hua-cás* signifies.[10]

Then the *taises* and other nobles began to sing and dance, and each one received a gift of importance which Quatlazape, in the name of his brother Maquinna and the princess, threw to them from the platform. One of the principal games of this solemn ceremony was the contest for which the ring that had been leveled for this purpose served as the arena. The prize that

[10] George Vancouver heard "Hua-cás" as "Wakash" both at Nootka and around on the Kwakiutl side of Vancouver Island at Cheslakee's village at the mouth of the Nimpkish River; from the similarity he gathered that the languages were related. Hence the term Wakashan for the linguistic family that comprises Kwakiutl and Nootka.

was offered to the winner was a shell,[11] and twenty or thirty na-ked athletes quickly presented themselves to vie for the honor of victory. From the top of the platform Quatlazape threw above them a small cylinder of wood which the contestants strove to catch in their hands. They snatched it from each other, using all their strength to seize it and keep it in their possession until the most vigorous or astute player obtained the final victory either by wearing down his opponents' ability to obstruct him, or by hiding [the piece of wood] with such skill as to make their per-sistence useless. Our sailors took part in this contest, and the prize which the winners received was always better than that given to the natives, since the latter received only shells and to the former were given excellent sea otter skins. Maquinna appreci-ated beyond measure our attending this celebration, and always testified to the pleasure he received from the fact that one of the chaplains and I danced in the presence of his daughter, the prin-cess.[12]

As soon as the ceremony was over, after having dedicated several days to the public rejoicing, Maquinna ordered Izto-coti-clemot to come down from the platform and took her to one of the looms in the best place in the house. "Now you are a woman, my daughter," he told her; "now you should not occupy your-self in anything except the obligations of your sex." With this the tender young girl began from that day to spin and weave, by her industrious conduct giving a lively rebuke to all those young ladies who do not have the rank of nobility and do not count idleness among the vices, and imitating, through the wise maxims of her education, the sisters of the Greek king who conquered all of Asia.

Before her period of menstruation, this girl came to visit us every day. She sang, danced, and passed the time happily, never

[11] Probably abalone.
[12] The Yale MS reads, "which he received from having seen one of the Chaplains and other individuals of the Botanical Expedition dance in the presence of and in honor of his daughter the Princess."

without a smiling face or failing to attend the festivities among all her relatives and servants. But afterward the gravity with which she handled herself surprised us all. She did not answer our greetings with more than a nod of her head, nor was she able to do more than smile shyly and speak one or two words. Our commandant enjoyed the friendship of Maquinna to the greatest degree that confidence can achieve, yet all his pleadings were not enough to persuade the chief to bring his daughter even one day to dine in our company. Whenever he spoke to him about the matter, [Maquinna] responded that his daughter was now a woman and could not leave the house.

I was finally able to find out that superstition had too great an influence in this conduct, since they believe that it is a grave sin against Qua-utz if the *taisa*, having seen the first blood which gives indication of her puberty, does not stay indoors for a period of ten months, eating little and only certain foods, because if she does the contrary she would be in danger of losing her life in punishment of her sin.[13] Our contact relaxed the vigor of this discipline somewhat, since during two visits which we made afterward she spoke to us with greater freedom. In the end, with permission from her father and accompanied by her stepmother Cla-sia-ca, she went to a small wooded area on the shore of the sea, from which she repeated her good-byes to us several times with very expressive signs.

---

[13] According to Drucker (Personal communication, December 11, 1967), Moziño has this backward—the pubescent's seclusion preceded the debut and potlatch. He interprets Moziño's observations to mean that the girl had already undergone her lengthy puberty seclusion and was allowed some freedom until time for the move to Copti where the potlatch could be given. Restrictions afterward were normal for young women of high rank before marriage. The final ceremonies of a girl's puberty rites and her period of seclusion are discussed by Drucker, *Northern and Central Nootkan Tribes*, pp. 140–42, and by Frances Densmore, *Nootka and Quileute Music* (Smithsonian Institution Bureau of American Ethnology Bulletin 124; Washington, D.C.: U.S. Government Printing Office, 1939), pp. 240–42.

# ARTICLE NO. 5

*Certain sacrifices performed by the natives; their occupation in fishing and the movement of their villages according to the seasons; administration of justice; some occupations like that of carpentry*[1]

T HE *tais* cannot sleep with his wives whenever he cannot see the disk of the moon entirely illuminated, and even then he has the obligation of abstaining if public calamities necessitate fasting and prayer. On such occasions he customarily retires to a mountain, accompanied by two or three of his domestic servants, who take along provisions of food for themselves. They are exempt from the law of abstinence with which the priest mortifies himself. The latter stretches himself out face upward with his arms crossed over his chest and remains in this same position for many hours. At the end of this he stands up and, by shouting, implores divine piety, frequently directing his requests to the dead *taises*, whose origin testifies that he is not lying and whose benevolence he always desires to preserve since with their protection he hopes they will see that they are of his blood and will

[1] The published version (Carreño, *Noticias de Nutka*, p. 39) includes "administration of justice" and "carpentry" in the chapter heading for Article No. 6. I have included them here because these subjects are treated in Article No. 5.

crown him with happiness. In this manner he is accustomed to maintain himself for two or three days without taking any food except a few herbs and a little water.

At other times the *tais* says his prayers inside his own house in order to ward off, by these means, the storms which impede the *meschimes* from going out to fish and to their other work. Enclosing himself in the large box or niche of which I spoke before, he hits the boards of first one side and then the other very forcefully with his hands and shouts his prayers at the top of his lungs. I was able to learn one of the prayers and as the result of intensive work present it here translated: *Cacatzu-o-co-majai; ja-quel, o javi-jlil-jlem-co-jaui clut-nas: Chimipeo tzepi-tizmo: Nachac-tu-tzo, manac-tzeptme-chaatla jahua cha-tlehuit zeja-qui. Yx-jo-ja quetl chu-atl-chatl, a caqui-mult-je, jaquetl clul-jas nac-hunas jaquetl.* ("Give us, Lord, good weather, give us life, do not allow us to perish, watch over us; deliver the Earth from its storms and its inhabitants from sickness; interrupt the frequency of the rains. Allow us clear days and serene skies.")

Afterward the *tais* remains in the most profound silence and the women approach his tabernacle. They call him repeatedly by name and offer him food, but he is deaf to their solicitations. If by chance he opens his lips, it is only to speak with renewed fervor, as he is carried away more and more each time with the force of his devoted enthusiasm.

I could not determine the motive for the celebration of a barbarous sacrifice, the execution of which is reserved to the most valiant prince. It consists of his going to the shore of a deep, fresh-water lake accompanied by two *meschimes*. He leaves his cape in the care of his assistants and, taking two pieces of the roughest pine bark in both hands, dives headfirst from a rock. After a short while, raising his face out above the water, he rubs his two cheeks, forehead, and chin vigorously with the said bark. He again submerges and repeats the same cruel ceremony as many times as he wishes to dissipate more and more the blood that spurts copiously from the injured parts. His spectators meanwhile flatter his ears with their reiterated applause.[2] Quatlazape served as victim and priest when we were on the island. His religious intrepidity was applauded by the acclamation of the two *meschimes* who, without ceasing, repeated these words: *Hiachacus*[3] *Quatla-zape*, "Quatlazape is a great man."

I believe that in these days they do not carry out human sacrifices, either because they know the proper abomination in which the custom was held by the Spanish, English, and Bostonmen, or perhaps because they do not have any victims for them other than their unfortunate prisoners.[4] The peace which they have enjoyed without interruption since the year [17]89 has not allowed them to take any [prisoners], and the few that remained as a result of previous wars have been of great use in trade. They sell them to the Spaniards, who have had the generosity to buy them, not in order to keep them in the sorry lot of slavery, but in order to educate them as sons and bring them to the bosom of the Holy Catholic Church.

A nation of fisherman can only settle properties which include the beaches and the adjoining waters that bathe them. And thus, the people of Yuquatl [Nootka], like all the other inhabitants of this archipelago, dispute with arms the right of fishing in their respective districts; and they believe that foreigners violate this public right when they sail into these areas for that purpose.[5] Since they draw their principal sustenance from the sea, they always inhabit the shores. They move their domiciles according to the scarceness or abundance of fish in one area or another, or

[2] This was a special ritual cleansing done by the chief in connection with whaling or to insure an abundance of fishing. The procedure was part of the "ritual cleansing-spirit quest." See Drucker, *Northern and Central Nootkan Tribes*, pp. 167–69.

[3] Also spelled Haschacus, Ascha-cups.

[4] See Article 2, p. 22.

[5] The members of the Moachat confederacy, unable to prevent Spanish occupation of Yuquatl, were as a result dislocated and deprived of their long-established rights.

because the season has caused them some difficulty. The scattered villages of Maquinna begin at Woody Point [Cape Cook] and are separated from each other by at least two or three miles. In one the government is in the charge of one of his brothers, and another is in the charge of his wives. As winter gradually approaches, they go to those villages which offer the greatest protection. The people from Woody Point go to the vicinity of Point Maquinna; those who were situated there go to Maquinnas; those from there to Copti; and finally all the rest to Tasis, where they pass the rigorous months of December and January. Tasis is a place situated on the large island of Quadra and Vancouver at the foot of some enormous mountains.[6] These serve as a barrier against the ferocity of the north wind, and their shores are bathed by the waters of a very protected channel that terminates in the same mountainous area.

The majority of the scattered lodges are reunited here; their inhabitants sustain themselves with provisions of dry fish which they have been conserving during the previous months. The *meschimes* spend the long nights singing and dancing around the blazing fires which they light as protection from the cold, and with the permission of the *taises* they abandon themselves to the excesses of frivolity.

In this same place [Tasis], the *taises* receive visits from their friends and allies the Nuchimanes, whose settlements are on the opposite side of the mountains and are separated from the eastern slope by three fresh-water lakes.[7] Communication between the lakes is by means of two channels, in the latter of which the current is extremely rapid and causes many canoes to be wrecked. In order to move their houses from one place to another of those re-

[6] Drucker notes that Tasis comes from the word *taci* meaning "doorway," and refers to the fact that one of two overland trails to Kwakiutl territory began there (*Northern and Central Nootkan Tribes*, p. 228).

[7] According to Drucker (Personal communication, December 11, 1967), Moziño's description is of the overland trail to the Nimpkish River, crossing Woss Lake, and demonstrates that the Nuchimanes equal Nimpkish.

ferred to, they join together three or more canoes by means of the planks which serve as walls. On top of these they usually transport all their furniture in only one trip, leaving only the supports and beams that served as the foundation of the building on the land they abandon. This could perhaps be the reason why, although they have seen in our settlements cabins that are better constructed and give greater shelter, whose principal materials they themselves have provided, they have not up to now yielded to the temptation to use them as a model.

I was able to learn very little of their civil and criminal administration; but from the little I did learn I understood that the former was purely economic and the latter was commonly arbitrary. There is so much consideration for the nobles that often the principal *tais* does not dare even to reprimand them with words.

The commoners by their condition are slaves, and only through the goodness of their masters do they at times receive treatment as sons. And since vices increase with desires, and desires increase with the luxuries of sophisticated nations, no one will say that I exaggerate when I affirm that the vices of these savages are very few when compared to ours. One does not see here greed for another man's wealth, because articles of prime necessity are very few and all are common. Hunger obliges no one to rob on the highways, or to resort to piracy along the coasts. In addition to the fact that they are very abstemious in their meals, everyone can partake indiscriminately of the fish or seafood he needs, and with the greatest liberty, in the house of the *tais*.

The uniformity of dress, according to the rank each holds, means that everyone's cape is safe in the hands of others. The trade with Europeans has allowed them to become acquainted with various things which they would have been better off without forever, conserving the primitive simplicity of their customs. Copper, which among them has the same value gold has to us, has introduced part of the misfortune greed always causes.

17. Cyprinus americanus? [*species unknown*]

18. Scomber? mahvinos [*species unknown*]

*19.* Lonicera nutkensis, *honeysuckle*

20. Campanula linearis, *harebell or bellflower*

21. Claytonia virginiana, *springbeauty*

22. Lilium kamschatkense, *Kamchatka lily*

23. Fumaria cuculata, *fulmitory*

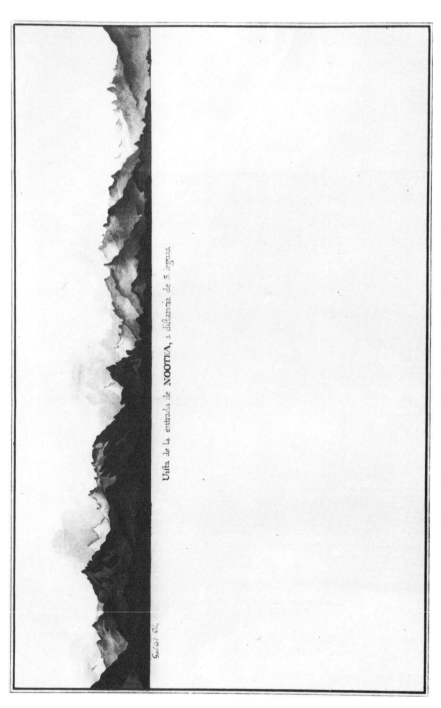

Vista de la entrada de **NOOTKA**, a distancia de 3 leguas.

Gabriel Gil.

24. *View of the entrance of Nootka Sound at a distance of three leagues*

Nevertheless, in order to restrain these offenses, Maquinna decreed the penalty of death to any of his men who might be convicted of robbing the Spanish ships. This same chief has at various times returned the trifles which his *meschimes* have stolen. Even their games are never for wager, but are a simple diversion by which they prove their greater agility in paddling, their strength in fighting, or their dexterity in hitting the mark in hunting.

Women are the only object that can compel them to frequent transgressions of the established order, and this offense would not be so prevalent if the commoners were all married. The man of this class who violates the conjugal bed of a *tais* gives his life as the penalty; the female accomplice is punished with whipping and banishment, with the obligation of submitting to all the hardships of a *meschimes*. If the adulterer is a prince, he suffers only banishment, after having seen the unfortunate object of his affections whipped in his presence.

The standard is not the same for women of the lower class. The *taises* themselves prostitute these women, especially to foreigners, in order to take advantage of the profit earned from this business. I learned that one of the most prominent *taises* always delivered his own wife when the reward that was offered seemed to him exceptional. But in general they exclude the *taisas*[8] when they wish to employ themselves in pandering, a role they do not consider ignominious.

This wantonness has surely been sad for those small settlements, which are gradually weakened by the ravages of venereal disease; within a few years it can ruin them so that the entire race will perish. I believe that today, adding up the total number of subjects belonging to each of the three *taises*, they do not comprise a group approaching two thousand persons. These, sterilized by this pernicious contagion, ought to fear the unfortunate fate

---

[8] The Spanish feminine form of *tais* (*taisa*) is used by Moziño to designate the wife of a *tais*.

of the people of Baja California, of whose race there scarcely remains one or two, the rest consumed by the raging syphilis which the sailors of our ships have spread among them.

The small number of men, and the simplicity of the life they lead, does not provide opportunity for many artisans or even for a variety of occupations. Those of the men are carpentry, fishing, and hunting; those of the women are spinning and weaving. They learn everything appropriate to their sex. Carpenters use only fire, shells, and flints as tools. In order to uproot a tree, they set it on fire at the base. Then they pull off the bark, and if they want to make boards they insert wedges in sections parallel to its axis using the same technique as that of the Mexicans in fashioning the narrow little boards which they call *tlajamanil*.[9] A beam has the entire thickness of the pine tree without the bark, and it requires no more work than uprooting it, cleaning it of the bark, and placing it on the site where it is needed. The construction of their boxes and canoes is work that demonstrates their great patience. [The canoes] are usually of a single piece, and in order to hollow out the tree from which they make them they apply fire gently on one side, scraping out the charred parts with their shell knives and thus wearing away the cavity until it has the dimensions they want to give it. When this has been accomplished they turn the tree over to its opposite side and in the same manner cut and shape it to form the keel. The drawing represents better than I can explain it the graceful lines they have.[10]

The canoes are extremely maneuverable, and the men who paddle them equally dexterous. The paddles serve also for steering since all the canoes lack a rudder. No matter from how far away a canoe is seen, and although from a distance the dress of

[9] Strips of wood used as shingles for roofs in rural areas of Mexico.

[10] Drucker (*Indians of the Northwest Coast*, pp. 73–74) describes the construction of a Nootkan canoe with an excellent illustration; see also Densmore, *Nootka and Quileute Music*, pp. 19–22. The drawing to which Moziño refers has not been found, although Plate 9 gives a general idea of the Nootkan canoe.

both sexes appears identical, one can nevertheless discern whether men or women are paddling because the paddles of the women are blunt at the tip, and those of the men so sharp that they use them to wound their enemies when these try to come aboard in naval battles.[11]

---

[11] Cook described their canoes as "very light, and their breadth and flatness enable them to swim firmly, without an outrigger—a remarkable distinction between the craft of all the American nations and that of the Southern Pacific Ocean. Their paddles are small and light, the shape in some measure resembling that of a large leaf, pointed at the bottom . . . the whole being about five feet long (Synge, ed., *Cook's Voyages*, p. 437).

# ARTICLE NO. 6

*Method of fishing for whales and sea otter and method of hunting; occupations of the women, and some arts they know*

FISHING is the branch of industry to which general necessity has forced these inhabitants to apply themselves. Consequently, they well know the seasons in which each kind of fish is abundant and the particular method that should be employed in catching it. In former days they had only fishhooks which they made from shells;[1] but at present these have been abandoned because of the great collection they have made of iron ones. Their nets are small and cannot be used except for catching the smallest fish.

They have another instrument, twenty feet long, four or five inches wide, and one-half inch thick, which is fitted with teeth more than two inches long for two-thirds of its length, the other part being left free to serve as a handle. Herring, and in general any fish come in schools, remain imprisoned here as in a trap.[2]

---

[1] Fishhooks were generally made of straight or slightly curved wooden shanks with bone or horn points. See Drucker, *Indians of the Northwest Coast*, p. 39.

[2] Cook said that the instrument was like an oar "about twenty feet long, four or five inches broad, and about half an inch thick" (Synge, ed., *Cook's Voyages*, p. 437). Drucker (*Northern and Central Nootkan Tribes*, p. 23)

[ 46 ]

Sardines are the fish found in greatest abundance, and their catch offers the most entertaining spectacle. A great many canoes join together and, forming a semicircle, close in the mouth of the port and all the places where these fish might escape. [The fishermen] vibrate long, thick poles underneath the water to frighten the fish and, gradually drawing their canoes closer together, each time form a smaller circle until they have corralled the fish in a very small cove, from which they pull them out quickly and in great numbers with nets, little baskets, and rakes.[3] They even gather them in their hands from the places where they are most thickly collected. At the conclusion of the fishing, the *tais*, or someone appointed by him, distributes a considerable portion to each village.[4] In shallow channels they drive in stakes which are tied with cattail leaves and serve as traps to imprison the fish.

Among all the types of fishing, none is more admired than that for the whale. A small canoe, with a keel of scarcely fifteen feet and a two-and-one-half-foot beam, manned by three or four men,

---

describes this herring rake as consisting of a "strip of yew wood, 10 to 12 feet long, 2 or 3 inches wide, and ½ inch thick. Sharp points were set about an inch apart along the distal third of one edge. Anciently the points were of bone. . . . The man with the rake knelt in the prow, wielding the implement like a paddle, but edgewise. He followed through on each stroke, bringing the rake behind him over the canoe and giving it a quick shake to detach the fish impaled on the points."

[3] According to Drucker (*Northern and Central Nootkan Tribes*, pp. 57–58), "Shiners (kȧqamhaiq) and a kind of perch (?) (ȧmȧnȧt) school up in coves during the latter part of the summer. They were caught by a kind of drive called satca'oph. A group of men formed a line of canoes across a small cove. They held fir boughs, weighted at the tips with stones, over the sides of the canoes, and worked in sideways until the fish were gathered close enough together to be taken with a (herring) scoop net or a herring rake. Another method of catching these fish was to pile a weir of stones across a shallow creek mouth, leaving an entryway. Both species run in the brackish creek mouths with incoming tide. When the tide turned, the entry was closed with branches. The ebb left the fish stranded against the weir." See Plate 9.

[4] The *tais*, whose power was derived from his property holdings, owned not only the entire village but the fishing places in the rivers and the sea and the hunting and gathering areas. The chief thus distributed fish and other food among the people of his village and of neighboring ones under his jurisdiction.

goes out to catch the most enormous animal that nature pro-
duces.[5] The inventive genius of man is always revealed in proportion to his needs, and that of these savages in the matter with
which we are dealing is not inferior to that of the most civilized
nations.

They thrust into the whale, with great force, a sharp harpoon
attached to a long and heavy shaft so that it will pierce more
deeply. This shaft is then recovered by means of a rope, and at
the same time they slacken another [rope], tied at one end to
the harpoon and at the other to an inflated bladder, which floats
over the water like a buoy, marking the place to which the wounded animal has fled during the short time in which it stays alive.
There is no catch which the natives solemnize more, nor from
which they obtain greater profit. The chief himself is present
during the distribution, and when this is done he gives a splendid
banquet to all the villages.[6]

I did not see the methods by which they capture sea otters. Because they have become so scarce, it is a very rare thing to encounter one in any part of that bay. Having observed that the
majority of skins are without holes, I suspect that they kill them
with sticks, watching closely for the chance of finding them
asleep on the large rocks; or they catch them with slip nooses
which are usually called snares.[7]

Hunting provides them with land animals and shore birds. For
this purpose nothing is worth more to them today than the gun,
and it is very clear that this has replaced, only to their advantage,
the ancient use of the arrow.

[5] Moziño is wrong. Whaling canoes were necessarily much larger to
stow lines and floats and were manned by a crew of eight. See Drucker,
*Central and Northern Nootkan Tribes*, pp. 51–55, and *Indians of the Northwest Coast*, pp. 45–49.

[6] Jewitt gives a good description of the special significance of whaling in
relationship to the power of the chief (Brown, ed., *Adventures of John
Jewitt*, pp. 123–27).

[7] According to Drucker (Personal communcation, December 11, 1967),
Moziño was mistaken since sea otter do not "haul up" on rocks like seals.

Since their dances often represent this kind of activity, I observed in one of them the preparation of nets and also the imitation of animals plunged into a pit covered over with slender canes that could be broken by the weight of the body. I have seen complete heads of bears and deer well-prepared for being placed over their own heads. This made me think that they follow the same strategy with which the Californians guarantee their shots by disguising themselves with the appearance of the beast they are trying to kill.[8]

The sedentary arts consist solely of spinning and weaving, and constitute the daily occupation of the women. In spinning, they have no equipment other than their muscles and fingers to unite the fibers of cedar [bark], wool, and otter hair. With these they first form a thick strand, which they afterward narrow and lengthen, winding it onto a small bar about one foot long which they turn above a small plank with the same dexterity and agility our Indian women use in their *malacates*.[9]

The looms for weaving textiles are very simple.[10] They hang the warp from a horizontal cane at a height of four and one-half feet from the ground, and with only their fingers, moving with swiftness, flexibility, and extraordinary deftness, they make up for all the tools that would make this work less cumbersome. They have patterns for making hats and capes; they begin both of them with a closely woven center, and weave the ends of the

---

[8] Alejandro Malaspina described this practice among California Indians during his expedition's visit to Monterey in 1791: "To kill the latter [deer] the Indians put on the stuffed head of an already killed deer; and hiding their bodies in the grass, they imitate the stance, appearance and look of the deer with such propriety that many are deceived until attracted to within range" (quoted from "California y Costas N.O. de America," MN, MS 330 by Cutter, *Malaspina in California*, p. 53). Drucker (Personal communication, December 11, 1967) indicates, however, that Moziño was wrong since "deerhead decoys" were not used, and that the headskins he saw were probably dance regalia.

[9] In Mexico, a spindle whorl; here a kind of spindle or bobbin.

[10] See C. F. Newcombe's notes on the looms used by the Nootkan Indians in 1792 (*Menzies' Journal*, pp. 154–55).

[ 49 ]

threads around the edges. For sleeping mats they use no more equipment than do our Indians of Xochimilco.[11] The mats are too coarse, either because the cattails do not lend themselves to finer work, or perhaps because they do not take much trouble in weaving them. Cured leather of all kinds is very good; the skins remain extremely soft and can be folded as easily as those of the most skillful tanners.

They work very little with metals. They cut copper into narrow strips, bend back the edges, and curve them to form bracelets and so forth; or without bending them they make the small cylinders which they hang from their ears and the ends of their hair. They lack whetstones upon which to sharpen their iron instruments, and thus are content to make a point by the force of their blows. They drill perfectly well the small snailshells and the blunted tips of Venus [dentalium] shells, of which they make the same use our ladies do of pearls. Their writing and painting are very crude.[12] Not only are these arts not in their infancy among them; to speak with exactness, they do not exist even in embryo.

[11] The Yale MS contains the note, "Town two leagues from Mexico in which they manufacture mats, which in New Spain are called *Petates*."

[12] See Bill Holm, *Northwest Coast Indian Art: An Analysis of Form* (Seattle: University of Washington Press, 1965); Robert Bruce Inverarity, *Art of the Northwest Coast Indians* (Berkeley and Los Angeles: University of California Press, 1967); and Erna Gunther, *Art in the Life of the Northwest Indians* (Seattle: Superior Publishing Company, 1966).

# ARTICLE NO. 7

*Concerning the language and its affinity with that of Mexico; the eloquent discourse of Prince Maquinna; of the rhetoric and poetry of the Nootkans, and of their dances*

THEIR language is the harshest and roughest I have ever heard; the pronunciation is done almost entirely with the teeth, each syllable being articulated by pauses.[1] The words abound in consonants, and the endings are often *tl* and *tz*. The middle and the beginning of words consist of very strong aspirations to which a foreigner cannot accustom himself except through much work and after long practice. I have so forgotten the Mexican [Nahuatl] language[2] that I find myself unable to

[1] The designation "Nootkan," originally applied to the Moachat by Cook, as noted above, is a linguistic one referring to a branch of the Wakashan stock. Within the Nootkan language there are three dialectic divisions: Nootka proper, spoken from Cape Cook to the east shore of Barkley Sound; Nitinat, used further south at Pacheena and Nitinat Lake; and Makah, used at Cape Flattery. Among the groups speaking Nootka proper, a major break occurred at Esteban Point just south of Nootka Sound; those north of this point showed a greater amount of cultural borrowing from their linguistically related neighbors, the southern Kwakiutl. See Edward Sapir, "Some Aspects of Nootka Language and Culture," *American Anthropologist*, XIII (1911), 15–28.

[2] The Yale MS reads, "The little instruction which I have had in the Mexican language makes me unable. . . ."

make an analogy with this one in a constructive way. To the ear both languages present a similarity in the word endings, and by just considering one or two sounds alone, I find some affinity between the two.[3]

In order to say "we go," the Mexicans use the word *tlato*, and the Nootkans, in order to say "go away," use *tlatlehua*. Knowledgeable persons can consult the small dictionary I have placed at the end,[4] in which I have attempted to write the words with letters which, when pronounced in Spanish, give a sound equivalent to that with which the Nootkan language enters my ears.[5] Anyone who takes into consideration the difficulty of representing by symbols the different actions of verbs conforming to all the

[3] Juan Eugenio Santelices Pablo, a linguistic expert of Mexico City, was asked by Viceroy Revilla Gigedo in 1791 to prepare a small dictionary uniting the four languages of Spanish, Mexican (Nahuatl), Nootkan, and Sandwich (Hawaiian) for use by Alejandro Malaspina. Santelices Pablo wrote that "no connection exists between those of Sandwich and Nootka, nor does either of them relate to the Mexican" (Santelices Pablo to Josef de Espinoza, Mexico, March 16, 1791 [letter of transmittal and dictionary], Additional MSS. No. 17631, Archives of the British Museum [London]).

[4] See below, p. 99. There were a number of vocabularies in existence at the time of Moziño's visit to Nootka with which he was undoubtedly familiar, although he does not give any specific credit. In the diary of Esteban José Martínez under the date of September 30, 1789, there appears a small dictionary "delivered to me by D. José Ingraham and translated into Castilian by our English interpreter Gabriel del Castillo with the addition of other words which we have acquired, because that which appears in the work of Captain Cook is defective in pronunciation." Haswell's First Log (Howay, ed., *Voyages of the "Columbia,"* pp. 102 ff.) includes a Nootkan-English vocabulary which can be compared with Captain Cook's in *Voyage to the Pacific Ocean*, II, 335–36, and III, 540 ff. Among the manuscripts in the Museo Naval appears a "Bocabulario de varias vozes que pronouncian los Indios en la Costa Septentrional de California, segun la obra de Cook" (Mn, MS 331); "Pequeño Bocabulario dada por D. Manuel Quimper de los havitantes comprendidos entre los 48 y 50 grados de latitud en su viaje al reconocimiento del Estrecho de Fuca el año 1790" (MN, MS 331); and a vocabulary similar to that of Moziño "prepared during the time of our establishment, the major portion of which is owing to [the work of] the said Don Pedro Alberni . . ." (MN, MS 468).

[5] The Yale MS reads, ". . . give a feeling, I mean sound [*den un sentido, digo sonido*] equal to that which entered my ears from the mouth of the Nootkan Indians and of travelers." It then omits the discussion of verb conjugation which completes the paragraph.

various tenses in which they function will easily realize the imperfection of those I have collected. I have given all of them the infinitive form although I understand that some are in the present perfect, others in the past, and others, finally, in the future. To the word *auco* I give the meaning "to eat," when it really means no more than "he eats." With this word I tried to begin to learn the pattern of its conjugation, but the only result of all my diligence was to observe the third person [singular and plural] of the present indicative tense, the three persons of the singular past perfect, and the second person of the imperative: "he eats," *auco*; "they eat," *auca*;[6] "I ate," *aucmiz*; "you ate," *auc*; "he ate," *aucmitis*; "you eat," *aucce*. On this occasion I observed that with some small variations they could be turned into negatives. *Huic-mutz* means "I did not eat"; *huic-mutitz*, "he did not eat." When an interrogative is formed, [the verb] is combined with the words of the question to form a single expression; for example, *A chitz-aco? A chichitl mic?* "Whose is this?" "To whom does it belong?"

The extensiveness of this language can be estimated by the degree of civilization this tribe has attained, since I think the rule is generally true that the wiser the nation, the richer is the language they speak. Consequently, that of Nootka is very poor, since it cannot have greater breadth than the ideas the Nootkans have been able to form.

Their system of numbering is by tens. All the numbers from one to ten have a particular name. Twenty is expressed among them by two times ten, thirty by three, and so on successively. I believe that it has never been necessary for them to count many thousands accurately, and consequently, when for some reason they are obliged to speak in very large numerical quantities, they represent them in an indefinite manner, repeating five, six, or seven times the word *ayo*, which means "ten."[7]

---

[6] There are variations in spelling among the several manuscripts, but the sound is the same.

[7] The dictionary included by Martínez (*Diario*, September 30, 1789) con-

The names of the measurements are merely those of the out-stretched hand, counting its size from the point of the little finger to that of the thumb [a span], and numbers of fingers across, which are used to express smaller amounts.

Since eloquence has always been considered the child of vivid passions, and since these are capable of firing the imagination of even these savages, it should not seem strange that I affirm its existence among these islanders, and in passing forestall those critics who are quick to claim that the speeches placed in the mouths of these savages by certain writers are false, as if in order to speak with enthusiasm, making use of the most moving figures of speech, it is necessary to attend the universities, to read books entitled "Rhetoric," and be ridiculous mimics of Marcus Tullius [Cicero]. To be eloquent, it is enough to follow freely the impulse of nature, whose mastery created the most celebrated orators of Greece.

I will never forget a discourse as exciting as it was poetic, which I heard Maquinna deliver on the occasion of satisfying our commander concerning a crime of which some had unjustly suspected him to be the author.[8] Four or five days before we left that port, the body of one of the cabin boys was found on a small mountain, covered with dagger wounds, naked, and without any flesh on the calves of his legs.[9] Near him was a handkerchief and a bloody

---

tains numbers one through ten and continues with twenty, thirty, forty, and so forth to one hundred. Haswell notes in his vocabulary that "They cannot count any higher than an Hundred" (Howay, ed., *Voyages of the "Columbia,"* p. 102).

[8] The Yale MS reads, "I will copy a discourse, as exciting as it was moving, made by Maquinna (the original of which I saw in the Diary of one of our travelers) on the occasion of satisfying our Spanish commander. . . ." Vancouver wrote in his journal for September 15, 1792: "Doubts arose whether this horrid act had been perpetrated by the natives or by a black man of most infamous character, who had deserted from the Spanish vessel about the same time the boy was first missed" (Meany, *Vancouver's Discovery of Puget Sound*, p. 322).

[9] Menzies reported the incident with the comment that the "small piece cut out of the Calf of each Leg" was probably caused by the contraction

English knife. Many assumed that Maquinna's Indians had committed this murder, induced perhaps by the chief himself in order to make use of the clothing and the flesh of the unfortunate young boy. This rumor ran through all the foreign vessels lying in the anchorage, and their respective captains promised to join with us to avenge this atrocity. Accordingly, the following day the Boston-man Ingraham[10] arrested two servants of Maquinna called Frijoles and Agustín, informed the Brigantine *Activo*, and asked for soldiers to transfer them to the stocks on that ship. Frightened by such an apparatus, they threw themselves into the water, where, despite their skill in swimming, they were overtaken by our launch, in which they were brought, with their hands tied, into the presence of Señor [Bodega y]Quadra. He was well satisfied of their innocence, since they had not been absent for even an instant on the night when the cabin boy was killed. For this reason he set them free, only charging them to entreat Maquinna on his behalf to attempt to determine who had been the aggressor.

Two days later that prince came and, with me serving as interpreter, explained himself to the commander in approximately these terms: "Frijoles and Agustín have informed me that Ingraham detained them on his ship in order to deliver them to the Spanish *meschimes*,[11] who brought guns to kill them if they attempted to escape from the bonds with which they tried to tie them, and who were going to put their feet in the stocks which are on board your ship. But they said that you, knowing that the charge of homicide against them was false, ordered them to be

---

"of the strong Muscles composing that part" and "would be of little consequence had it not been afterwards urged as proof that the Natives who were supposed to be the Murderers were Cannibals & cut out these pieces for the purpose of eating them" (Newcombe, ed., *Menzies' Journal*, p. 122).

[10] Joseph Ingraham, commander of the brigantine *Hope* from Boston.

[11] The Yale MS adds the note, "This is what he called the Spanish soldiers and sailors."

untied and allowed to go free to Tasis; and that your same *mes-chimes*, upon leaving mine, told them that I was the one who had plotted this crime.

"I believe that you are not convinced of this; that you realize that Maquinna has a thousand obligations to be your friend. You have given me much copper; because of you I had many shells to distribute at the celebration of the first menstruation of Apenas. Yours are the cloth, beads, coat of mail, instruments of iron, glass windowpanes, and many other things with which I am provided. Our mutual trust has reached the point of our both sleeping alone in the same room, a place in which you find yourself without arms or people to defend you. I could have taken your life if my friendship were capable of betrayal. One thinks very lowly of me and of my dignity if he imagines that, seeking to break a friendship, I would order the murder of a boy less able to defend himself than if he were a woman.

"Do you presume that a chief such as I would not commence hostilities by killing the other chiefs and placing the force of my subjects against that of their *meschimes*? You would be the first whose life would be in great danger if we were enemies. You well know that Wickinanish has many guns as well as powder and shot; that Captain Hana[12] has more than a few, and that they, as well as the Nuchimanes, are my relatives and allies, all of whom, united, make up a number incomparably greater than the Spanish, English, and Americans together, so that they would not be afraid to enter combat.

"What clothing did the boy have which would excite—I do not say my greed—but that of any of my servants? Have not your brothers (thus he called all of us)[13] on various occasions been alone in my house, as well as in those of Quioco-masia and Nana-

[12] Captain Hana was an Indian (Chief Cleaskinah) who exchanged names as a token of friendship with Captain James Hanna of the *Sea Otter* in 1785–86; this was a cultural trait among groups of the Northwest.
[13] The Yale MS reads, "Thus they called the Naval Officers."

quius, well dressed, with watches and other curious adornments? What evil has been done to them? Who of my people has insulted them in any way? Have not you yourself gone accompanied by few of your men and found only that the multitude of my subjects surrounded you with the purpose of making the liveliest demonstrations of friendship? How then can you permit your men to speak unworthily of me and allow Ingraham to assert that Frijoles and Agustín killed this boy?

"Make them all know that Maquinna is your true friend, and that he is so far from harming the Spanish, that they find him quick to avenge the injury they have just received, by my surmise, from the hands of the treacherous ones of Itz-coac. You know the power and daring of my brother Quatlazape and my relative Nat-zape. If you will lend me your launch,[14] with four or six swivel-guns, I will send them both with the most valiant of my *meschimes* to destroy those bandits and clear them out of the opposite coast. You can send whichever of your men you wish, so that they and mine, as well as our enemies, will know that Maquinna is the same as Quadra, and Quadra is the same as Maquinna."

They are all generally fond of singing, either because the music enters into part of their rituals, or because it constitutes one of the demonstrations of their courtly ceremonies.[15] Their natural voices create the harmony in unison on the octave. They are accompanied, in place of bass, by a noise which the singers make on some boards with the first solid object they find, and by some wooden rattles whose sound is similar to that of the Mexican

[14] The published version of *Noticias de Nutka* has the Spanish word *lanza* (lance), whereas the Revilla Gigedo MS and Yale MS read, correctly, *launcha* (launch).

[15] Densmore (*Nootka and Quileute Music*) and Drucker (*Northern and Central Nootkan Tribes*) list songs for no fewer than twenty-five occasions, including those connected with whaling, hunting, house raising, puberty rites, inheritance, love, marriage, war, victory, potlatch ceremonies, supernatural beings, mourning, weather, and so forth.

*ayacaztles* [Aztec gourd rattles].[16] One of the singers constantly gives the tone and all the others follow it successively, forcing their voices unevenly, in almost the same manner customary in the Gregorian chant of our churches. From time to time one of the musicians abandons the chant and gives enormous shouts, repeating the theme of the song as if in summary.

These are ordinarily hymns to celebrate the beneficence of Qua-utz, generosity of their friends, and good relations with their allies. This noble purpose of music and poetry ought to serve as an example to us, who flatter ourselves that we have been born in cultured countries and educated in the bosom of the true religion. One day Quio-comasia heard some stanzas sung at a certain meeting which we had with the English and the natives. At the conclusion of the song he asked me what had been its subject, to which I replied that it was the absence of a lady. Afterward other Spaniards and Englishmen sang their respective songs, and the gathering was brought to a close with a beautiful anacreontic ballad, the grace of which enhanced the soft and melodious voice of the young Irishman who sang it. The *tais* kept asking me the meaning of each piece. The first were purely love songs (I told him), and what he had just heard was a eulogy to wine and pretty girls. To this he replied, "Do not the Spanish or the English have a God, since they celebrate only fornication and drunkenness? The *taises* of Nootka sing only to praise Qua-utz and ask for his help."

This same chief, hearing us play some of our instruments, assured me that he did not like them very much because they seemed similar to the songs of birds, which please the ear but do not require understanding. Another prince (Nana-quius) criticized our trills and all the music in which the soft languidness of the notes stood out. He said that the person who trilled appeared

[16] The wooden rattles of the Nootkans were usually carved in the form of a bird; their only other musical instruments were rattles, drums, and whistles.

to be shivering from cold and the others to be singing with an air of drowsiness. This did not surprise me, nor would it be a reason that would make me condemn the rusticity of these savages, knowing the fate the celebrated inventor of the achromatic tetrachord suffered in Sparta. I recognize in the people of Nootka thoughts more virile than those which music usually inspires in us—the excessively tender ones to which we are accustomed.

But, in spite of everything, I noticed that among the commoners, or *meschimes*, the use of music and poetry was very much profaned. One night they presented a spectacle for us which surely exceeded the indecent pantomimes of the ancient Greeks and Romans; and I have information that they spend all the nights in Tasis during the winter in this kind of recreation. Many times the spectators of this dissolute opera are these same *taises*, who scruple only not to mingle their voices in the obscene songs.

Up to now I have used the word poetry because I am convinced that they actually have it, although I have not been able to understand the kinds of meters of which their verses are comprised. They certainly have several, granting that they fill out their metric construction as completely as we do ours. The style varies according to the nature of the theme. In their pantomimes I noticed that they made use of brilliant expressions, [giving] vivid and witty portrayals, which I do not describe here in detail because they are the most lascivious that one can imagine. The songs of the *taises*, I thought, were filled with enthusiasm, as much because the very object to which they were directed naturally required elevation in all the ideas, as has been observed, as because they themselves were enraptured by their singing. I was able to understand very little about the meaning of the phrases, despite the pains my great friend Nana-quius took to explain this material to me with as much clarity as possible.

The dances are very varied, but in all of them the harmony that is apparent in their songs is less evident. The most common is a vigorous heel-tap producing inharmonious steps and improvised turns. When the chief dances alone, he often carries in his hand one of the valuable objects which he intends to present at the function. It is the custom for many to dance at one time, and in this case one observes much variety in the movements, many different[17] positions, and greater regularity in rhythm. Everything is meaningful, and the whole represents a kind of pantomine. In the martial dance the participants are presented armed with bows, arrows, and guns; the music is then more vigorous, and their faces and all their gestures indicate only fierceness. They sometimes disguise themselves with skins, and heads of bears and deer, or with masks of wood which represent in a huge size the figure of some aquatic bird whose movements, as well as those of the hunter who snares it, they attempt to imitate. The fall of the bear into a net, its death, or that of a deer pierced through the heart with an arrow, are things represented so naturally, and so in time with the music, that they cannot fail to excite admiration.

Decency compels me to omit the detailed description of the obscene dances of the *meschimes* because the movements with which they carry them out are extremely scandalous, especially in the dance of the man impotent because of age and of the poor man who has not been able to marry.[18] The women dance gracelessly without moving away from the place where they are. They make slow turns, raising first one arm and then the other while inclining the body toward the opposite side. They rarely indulge in this diversion, and never in front of persons with whom they do not have some familiarity.

[17] The Yale MS has the word *difíciles* (difficult).
[18] Drucker comments: "The humor of these sketches was heavy at best; in some instances they were frankly obscene. The 'obscene dances' that scandalized Mozino in 1791 . . . were undoubtedly age-grade club performances. There was no esoteric motivation behind these skits. Their aim was amusement only" (*Northern and Central Nootkan Tribes*, p. 404).

# ARTICLE NO. 8

*Concerning their chronology and method of counting the days, months, and years; origin of the population of the island and the small trade of the natives; the arrival of a Spanish ship in 1774, and of Captain Cook's in 1778; commerce in sea otter skins established by the English Captains Gore, King, Hanna, and Meares; later voyages with the same purpose from Ostend and Boston, etc.*

T HEIR chronology is filled with obscurity, either because of the limited understanding we can have of the events that mark the beginnings of their epochs, or perhaps because of their neglecting to arrange their calendars with uniformity. The coming of Qua-utz in the canoe of copper is the first event from which they begin to count their years; but since the number of months, as well as of intercalary days, is computed by several methods, their years cannot be even approximately compared with our centuries. To this is added a new difficulty—the indefinite method with which they express a long series of days, months, and years. The most enlightened persons divide the year into fourteen months, and each month into twenty days. They then add several intercalary days at the end of each month, the number of which varies and is determined by the importance of the object which characterizes each month for them.

The month of July, which they call *Satz-tiz-mitl* and is the first of their year, has more than its ordinary twenty days. It contains as many intercalary days as the abundant supply of sole, tuna, cod, bass, and so forth lasts. The month that follows, comprising part of our August, is called *Tza-quetl-chigl* and has hardly any intercalaries. *Inic-coat-tzimil* [September] is the month set aside for the cutting of lumber which, as I have said, is done by burning the trunk of the pine at its base. For this reason the word *inic*, which means "fire," enters into the composition of the name. Fish are very scarce during the three months of *Eitz-tzul*, *Mamec-tzu*, and *Car-la-tic* [October, November, and December], and this period of scarceness preceding the winter, whose rigor is experienced in *Ajumitl*, *Uat-tzo*, and *Uya-ca-milks* [January, January/February, February], lasts through all three months. These months terminate near the middle of our February, which is the time when *Aya-ca-milks* [March] begins and the great sardine [herring] catch is celebrated.

The month of *Orcu-mi-gl* [April] is known for its abundance of ducks and seagulls. The following month, *Ca-yu-milks* [May], is solemnized with major functions; in it they fish for whales almost every day and make the collection of oil for the whole year. Finally, in *Ca-huet-mitl* and *Atzetz-tzimitl* [May and June], they harvest daily the fruits, roots, stems, leaves, and flowers of those plants mentioned at the beginning. The last of these months terminates almost exactly at the time of the vernal solstice [equinox].[1]

[1] Drucker gives the meaning of the Nootkan names of each month as: July, Wasp moon; August, Spring salmon (run) moon; September, Dog salmon moon; October, Rough sea moon; November, Elder sibling; December, Younger sibling; January, No (food getting) for a long time (?) moon; February, Bad weather moon; February, False (spawning) moon; March, Herring spawn moon; April, Geese moon; May, Stringing (berries) moon; June, Salmonberries moon (*Northern and Central Nootka Tribes*, pp. 115–16). The Nootkan names given by Moziño are very close in sound

The governments of the *taises* also make a kind of calendar upon which their special festivals are noted by months and days and by which the natives regulate their dates; but since the duration of these is calculated in accordance with their ordinary measurements of time, there always exist the same doubts, and one finds the road to penetrate the ancient history of this nation filled with obstacles.

In order to appear less rude in trying to learn the time, more or less, when this island was settled, I used the method of computing the ages of the *taises* and their ancestors. I presumed there had been some longevity among them because of the robust health which the fathers of Tlu-pana-nutl and Quio-comasia enjoy today, since the first is almost ninety years old, and the second not less than seventy. In this manner, according to the memory which they themselves have of their grandfathers, and supposing a difference of only twenty years from generation to generation, I found that they could call to mind some wars which took place approximately two hundred years ago. From there on all is lost in obscurity.

Since these wars, they say, were always with the Tlaumases, and since this name is applicable to all the nations that live on the other shore of the sea, it was impossible for me to establish historical exactitude about such indefinite objects. Any person who gains enough familiarity with their language to understand the songs in which the *taises* celebrate the deeds of their ancestors could with time instruct the curious about innumerable passages which would perhaps be interesting.

The kinship ties with the Nuchimanes and the princes' custom of marrying women of this tribe have resulted in the long-standing commercial relations between these villages. Through the agency of the Nuchimanes, the Nootkans extended their

---

to those listed by Drucker but are one month off in some cases. The months I have inserted in brackets are from Drucker's list. Moziño's are listed in Appendix A.

trade up to Bucareli Inlet and probably up to Queen Charlotte Island, in addition to the trade which they certainly have had, and now have, with the continent, across the strait of Juan de Fuca. They told me of having seen, after a trip of several days, a certain class of women[2] who had, under their natural mouth, an additional one that held a small stick of wood, and these, for certain, are not found except in the northern countries which I have just cited.[3]

The wool they intertwine with the cedar fibers is of a quadruped that is not found anywhere on the island, and if by chance it is the buffalo, as I have suspected, it is surely the one that abounds in the north of our most remote possessions of New Mexico.[4] When Captain Cook saw the Nootkans for the first time, he found that they already had a knowledge of iron and copper,[5] and it appears indisputable that they acquired these metals by trading on the continent with other nations which came to make exchanges [at a place] which, according to Captain [George] Vancouver, is no more than four hundred miles to the

[2] The Yale MS notes at this point: "Bucareli Inlet, which is in 55 degrees 18 minutes North latitude and 32 in longitude, is where they are accustomed to using the little wooden stick, according to the report of the expedition which Don Juan Francisco de la Bodega y Quadra made in the company of other commanders in the year 1779; these Indian women have good features and some an outstanding whiteness, but the piece of wood about two fingers wide which they put in their lower lip makes them ugly. It is the mark of married women."

[3] The labret, used by the northern Kwakiutl at Bella Bella and also by the Kitimat, Tsimshian, Haida, and Tlingit Indians, was described by almost all the early travelers (La Pérouse, Portlock and Dixon, Malaspina, and others). See Aurel Krause, *The Tlingit Indians*, translated by Erna Gunther (Seattle: University of Washington Press, 1956), pp. 96–98.

[4] It is unlikely that the wool was from buffalo; it was probably from mountain goats.

[5] John Ledyard wrote that "it was generally thought that they [some roughly wrought knives] came from a great distance and not unlikely from Hudson's-Bay" (Munford, ed., *Ledyard's Journal*, p. 77). Drucker (Personal communication, December 11, 1967) suggests that iron (small bits used for blades) did not come from Hudson's Bay but originally by native trade routes around the the northern rim of the Pacific. The Bering Strait Eskimo had iron from the Punuk period (ca. A.D. 1000).

east of a port in which he was anchored inside the strait. I do not have its name at present.[6]

To the south they appear not to have gone farther than the Island of Tutusi [Cape Flattery][7] and Port of Nuñez Gaona [Neah Bay],[8] to this point the same language is spoken with very little difference from that at 51°. Textiles, skins, whale oil, and canoes were apparently the articles they exchanged in their commerce, which indisputably must have been desultory since it was carried out among nations more or less supplied with the same products. In the year [17]78 the aspect of things changed entirely. For that part of America it was the beginning of a memorable epoch. Captain [James] Cook gave them some copper, and his crew bought a number of sea otters in exchange for pieces of this metal, knives, fishhooks, glass beads, and other trifles. The natives believed that they had succeeded in unloading their merchandise at a very advantageous price. In effect they had, considering the circumstances of that time, because they tripled their small capital by means of the copper which, leaving the hands of the Nootkans, began to disperse itself throughout almost all the Archipelago.

By the year 1774, these islanders had already seen a Spanish ship commanded by First Pilot Don Juan Pérez,[9] who anchored at the point which he himself called San Estevan and which Cook

[6] The Yale MS reads," . . . and whose name I do not know because it is not contained in the Diaries which have served as the source of this report."

[7] Tutusí was the name of the chief of the Makah Indians (the Tatootche of Meares and Tootoosch of Jewitt) and was applied to the point now known as Cape Flattery as well as present-day Tatoosh Island.

[8] Puerto de Nuñez Gaona was named by Manuel Quimper on August 1, 1970, after Manuel Nuñez Gaona, a rear admiral in the Spanish navy who died in 1813. Its present name Neah Bay apparently came either from the Indian word *dia,* meaning "far under water," or from the name of an early chief, Deeaht, sometimes pronounced "neeah" by the Clayoquots and Nitinats.

[9] "Continuación del Diario que formó el alférez graduado de Fragata Don Juan Pérez, Primer Piloto del Departmento de San Blas, con la titulada 'Santiago' alias 'la Nueva Galicia' de su mando . . . a explorar la costa Septentrional y su regreso . . . ," August 26, 1774, AGI, Estado 38.

afterward named Arrecifes. The sight of this ship at first filled the natives with terror, and even now they testify that they were seized with fright from the moment they saw on the horizon the giant "machine" which little by little approached their coasts. They believed that Qua-utz was coming to make a second visit, and were fearful that it was in order to punish the misdeeds of the people. As many as were able hid themselves in the mountains, others closed themselves up in their lodges, and the most daring took their canoes out to examine more closely the huge mass that had come out of the ocean. They approached it timorously, without sufficient courage to go aboard, until after awhile, attracted by the friendly signs by which the Spanish crew called them, they boarded the ship and inspected with wonder all the new and extraordinary objects that were presented to them. They received a number of gifts and in return gave the captain some otter skins. In his diary, the original of which I have read, it states that neither he nor any of his sailors went ashore, and it can be clearly inferred from it that neither did they examine the ports at a distance of five leagues to the north which would have supplied them with much relief. They finally set sail southward, without even surveying exactly the bearing of the coast, contenting themselves with merely determining the latitude of that entrance, which they called San Lorenzo. They afterward missed, among other things, some spoons, which had naturally excited the greed of the natives, in whose possession Cook found one of them four years later.[10]

This daring and wise navigator [Cook], looking for a passage

---

[10] Esteban José Martínez in his *Diario* on May 5, 1789, mentioned that Maquinna showed him the shells which Martínez had given him in 1774 when "he came to the port with Juan Péréz in the *Santiago*," and the Nootka chief also reported that "the Indian who had robbed him [Martínez] of the two silver spoons (those which were referred to by Captain Cook in his work) had died some time before." For the complete diary of Martínez' voyage with Pérez see "Viaje executado por el Piloto Estevan José Martínez en la Fragata *Santiago* . . . a la altura de 55 grados norte . . . en 24 dias del mes de Henero de 1774," AGI, Guadalajara 516.

by sea to the Atlantic along the Northwest Coast of America, discovered Esperanza Inlet and from there observed [the inlet] of San Lorenzo at a distance; to this he gave the name of King George Sound.[11] He directed his course toward it and dropped anchor in a small port, until now called Cook, situated on the coast of Yuquatl, six or seven leagues distant and facing the large rock on which today we have located our battery. With boats and launches Cook explored part of the nearby channels as well as the port [of Nootka] which has been so frequented in recent years.

I do not know through what error this island has been given the name of Nootka, since these natives do not know the word and assure me that they had never heard it until the English began to trade on the island. I suspect that the source of this mistake was the word *Nut-chi*, which means mountain, since what Cook called "Nootka" has never among these islanders had any name other than Yuquatl.[12]

This island would perhaps have followed the obscure fate of many others—being noticed only by geographers—if the skins which the sailors of the *Resolution* and *Discovery* diligently gathered had not been sold at such high prices in Canton and been insufficient to satisfy the desire the Chinese showed for sea otter skins. This excited the greed of the crews to such a point that the consummate prudence of Captains Gore and King, successors

---

[11] Cook, *Voyage to the Pacific Ocean*, II, 288.

[12] Martínez wrote that "the name of Nutka, given to this port by the English, is derived from the poor understanding between them and the natives . . . Captain Cook's men, asking [the Indians] by signs what the port was called, made for them a sign with their hand, forming a circle and then dissolving it, to which the natives responded Nutka, which means to give way [*retroceder*]. Cook named it in his Diary "entrada del Rey Jorge o de Nutka," and the rest of the ships have known it by the latter, which is Nutka, for which reason they have forced the Indians also to know it by that name; nevertheless, at first the new name always seemed strange; the true name by the natives is *Yuquat*, which means *for this*" (*Diario*, September 30, 1789). Meany (*Vancouver's Discovery of Puget Sound*, pp. 45–46) quotes Belgian missionary Father A. J. Brabant that *noot-ka-eh* is a native verb meaning "go around" and surmises that the Spaniards confused the word for the name of the Nootka village and thus adopted it for the harbor.

to Cook and Clerke, was not enough to repress the mutinous actions by which they were threatened in case they, as leaders, did not agree to return to America and take on a sizable cargo of furs. The spirit of these captains was attuned more to glory than to pecuniary interests, and they finally had the good fortune to dispel the avaricious thoughts of their subordinates and to inspire them with ideas of honor.[13]

Furthermore, Gore and King did not lose sight of the advantages to their nation which could result from the addition of this new branch of commerce. From Asia they began to encourage their compatriots to promote it, describing to them its ease, swiftness, and advantages. In England itself they publicized the project, and it was not received indifferently by those active and industrious businessmen. Captain Hanna was the first who navigated this coast with the sole purpose of trading in furs. When he arrived in Nootka, the natives approached his ship without the least fear, entered it, and stole various things.[14] They angered Hanna by this, and he ordered that a shot be fired to serve as a warning to those who followed.

John Meares made two trips with the same purpose, enriching himself more and more each time with the considerable earnings he was extracting.[15] He says that he purchased from Maquinna

[13] After the death of Cook in Hawaii, Clerke became commander of the expedition and the ships sailed northward to Kamchatka and the Arctic Sea looking for the the Northwest Passage. Clerke died in July, 1779, and Lieutenants John Gore and James King assumed command of the *Resolution* and *Discovery*, respectively. The ships then sailed for Canton, where they anchored in December; the officers and seamen sold their remaining otter skins for about two thousand pounds. The crew wanted to return to the Northwest Coast and even threatened mutiny, but the expedition returned to England in 1780 by way of the Cape of Good Hope. See Cook and King, *Voyage to the Pacific Ocean*, III, 437.

[14] Captain James Hanna's sixty-ton brigantine *Sea Otter* reached Nootka in August, 1785. The natives briefly attacked his small force of twenty men, but afterward became friendly and willing to trade. Hanna sold 560 sea otter skins obtained in that year from the Indians for $20,600 (Bancroft, *History of the Northwest Coast*, pp. 173–74).

[15] Meares arrived in Nootka Sound on May 13, 1788. See Meares, *Voyages*

the land adjoining the north side of this prince's village, which at that time occupied the same site on which the Spanish establishment is found today.[16] Maquinna denies this fact, as is clear from a public declaration he made at the request of Don Juan Francisco de la Bodega y Quadra, in the presence of Captains James Magee and Don Juan de Barros Andrade, Dr. Howell, the priest Don Joseph Jiménez, and the pilot Don Salvador Menéndez, with me serving as interpreter, since I understood the language of the various witnesses.[17] The fact is that Meares built his cabin on the land which he claimed to have purchased, that he constructed a sloop and planned to establish his trading post there.

[Captain Charles William] Barkley brought the Emperor Joseph II into this trade. He left from Ostend, commanding the *Imperial Eagle*, and investigated the entrance of Fuca, which up to then he had thought to be mythical. He lost some of his men, whom he had imprudently ordered into the launch, at the hands of the savages. He was in Nootka and continued his expedition further to the north.[18] At the same time, Captains Portlock and

---

*Made in the Years 1788 and 1789 from China to the North-West Coast of America.*

[16] According to Meany (*Vancouver's Discovery of Puget Sound*, p. 28), Meares immediately purchased a small tract of land at Friendly Cove from Maquinna for two pistols. There he built a house for his workmen and stores which he promised to give to Maquinna when he was through with it.

[17] Bodega y Quadra wrote in his journal: "Desiring to confirm in as authentic a manner as possible the granting of the land which Chief Maquinna made in favor of the Spaniards and which they occupy today in Nootka, it was appropriate that the said chief repeat his declaration in the presence of Dn. Santiago [James] Magee, Captain of the Boston frigate *Margaret*, Dn. Juan Barros Andrade, Captain of the Portuguese brigantine *San Jose Fenix*, Dr. John Howell, professor in arts at the University of Cambridge, as well as before Br. [Bachiller, i.e., Bachelor of Arts] Dn. José Jimenez, Chaplain of the Goleta *Activa* and Dn. Salvador Menéndez, First Pilot of the Royal Navy; consequently, the said Chief was asked by D. Jose Moziño, naturalist of the expedition under my command who acted as interpreter, about the sale which he had made to Mr. Meares, and he [Maquinna] answered that he had done no such thing with the word *Huic* . . ." ("Viaje de 1792.").

[18] Barkley (or Barclay) left Ostend November 23, 1786, and reached Nootka Sound in June, 1787. He apparently discovered the Strait of Juan

Dixon of the frigate *King George* and the packet boat *Queen Charlotte* followed the same course.[19] The second of these captains had come as a blacksmith on Cook's last voyage and always claimed that he had a special talent for navigation. When he separated himself from his commander, Portlock, in Prince William Sound, he discovered the island which he named Queen Charlotte, for his packet boat, and on which he was supplied with many excellent furs.

The Americans, whose diligence sought to exceed that of their ancient progenitors, did not propose to be left without a part of this lucrative trade. [John] Kendrick left from Boston commanding the *Columbia Rediviva*, and [Robert] Gray, under his orders, commanding the sloop *Washington*.[20] The latter penetrated nearly ten leagues into the Strait of Fuca before anyone else, but he did not make a complete circuit in his voyage as Meares supposed. The former [Kendrick], for ten guns and a little powder, bought a piece of land in Maquinnas on which to spend the winter.[21] He gained the friendship of the natives as no one else had, continually giving them presents, entertaining them with fireworks,

---

de Fuca in July of that year. Barkley remained for three months on the Northwest Coast trading for furs and spent some time at Nitinat, southeast of the Spanish Archipelago of Carrasco, in Barkley Sound.

[19] See George Dixon, *A Voyage Round the World but more particularly to the North-West Coast performed in 1785, 1786, 1787 and 1788 in the King George and the Queen Charlotte: Captains Portlock and Dixon* (London: George Goulding Publisher, 1789).

[20] See Howay, ed, *Voyages of the "Columbia,"* and "Voyages of Kendrick and Gray in 1787–90," *Oregon Historical Quarterly*, XXX (June, 1929), 89–94.

[21] The actual deed read: "To all persons to whom these presents shall come: I Macquinnah the chief, and with my other chiefs, do send greeting: Know ye that I, Macquinnah of Nootka Sound, on the north-west coast of America, for and in consideration of ten muskets, do grant and sell unto John Kendrick, of Boston, commonwealth of Massachusetts, in North America, a certain harbor in said Nootka Sound, called Chastacktoos . . . with all the land, rivers, creeks, harbors, islands, etc., within nine miles north, east, west and south of said harbor, with all the produce of both sea and land appertaining thereto . . . " (Senate Document, 32d Congress, 1st Session, *Report of Committee*, No. 335 [1852], p. 20).

speaking their language, wearing their clothes, and, in a word, adapting himself to all their customs. I cannot say whether it was self-interest or rivalry with the English that suggested to the Americans the perverse idea of teaching the savages the handling of firearms—a lesson that could be harmful to all humanity. He [Kendrick] gave Maquinna a swivel gun; he furnished Wickinanish with more than two hundred guns, two barrels of powder, and a considerable portion of shot, which [the Indians] have just finished using on the unhappy sailors of Captains Brown and Baker.[22]

[22] See Article 1, p. 16.

# ARTICLE NO. 9

*Voyage of the Spanish Commandant Don Esteban Martínez, by whom the Port of Nootka was taken; imprisonment of a Portuguese captain later given his freedom; disagreement between Martínez and the English Captain Colnett; and the violent death of Prince Quelequem*

IN 1789 the Spanish entered Nootka in the frigate *Princesa* and the packet boat *San Carlos* proceeding from San Blas; the commandant of the expedition was First Pilot Don Esteban Martínez.[1] They found no other ship there except the *Iphigenia Nubiana* commanded by the Portuguese [Francisco José] Viana, who immediately raised the flag of his nation. Martínez took possession of the port in the name of His Catholic Majesty with the customary formalities, without encountering resistance or receiving any protest from the captain of the Portuguese ship or from his purser [William] Douglas, of English nationality,[2] who, according to what Meares says, was his agent for the trade in furs.

By virtue of the authority which he justly believed himself to

[1] See Martínez, *Diario*, May 5, 1789.
[2] Martínez refers to Douglas as a native of Scotland.

[72]

hold, Martínez asked the Portuguese captain for his passports and orders and, provoked by some expressions in these papers which he did not understand well, had him arrested and confiscated his ship with all of its cargo. A clearer interpretation that was later made of the clauses that seemed wrong to the Spanish captain moved him to set his prisoner free and give him without further ado everything that had been seized.[3] According to the testimony of this same merchant, which is attached to the documents Sr. [Bodega y] Quadra has sent to the government, he not only did not lose anything during the days of his imprisonment, but received considerable aid toward the security of his ship and subsistence of his crew.[4]

The Boston-men Kendrick and Gray appeared at this time, and since their only purpose was trade, they had no motive for disagreement. They were able to establish such perfect harmony with the commandant of the port [Martínez] that even today they profess to be most ardent friends, and carry out this role with fre-

[3] Robert Haswell described the events of May 5, 1789, in the log of the *Columbia* as follows: "Don Martinaz now demanded Captain Douglass' papers and from what pretence I know not said they were false and made the vessel his prize . . . the officer and Seamen of the Ephagena, were kept prisoners for several days when on a more critical examination of the ships papers it was found that they could not detain the vessel with propriety, and she was delivered up to the former commanders upon conditions that should the court of Spain demand her as a prize she was to be delivered up and as the Ship was in want of cordage cables sails and in short almost every Nesecery that was proper on a passage of such duration with these Don Martenaz supplied them and took Bills on their owner and in party pay the Schooner NW American was to be delivered to him as soon as she should arrive—everything being settled thus Captain Douglas sailed for China" (Howay, ed., *Voyages of the "Columbia,"* p. 101).

[4] In answer to Bodega y Quadra's request, the Americans Robert Gray and Joseph Ingraham wrote the Spanish commandant a letter, dated August 3, 1792, explaining the events that had taken place at Nootka Sound in May, 1789, when Martínez arrived. They declared that while the *Iphigenia* was in possession of the Spaniards it was put in complete order for sea, its rigging and sails repaired, anchors and cables replaced, and so forth, and that the officers and crew were supplied with every kind of necessary provision (Bodega y Quadra, "Viaje de 1792," and Howay, ed., *Voyages of the "Columbia,"* p. 475).

quent defenses of the absent one, an opinion rejected by the other navigators[5] who frequent that port.

Finally the English Captain James Colnett arrived in the packet boat *Argonaut*,[6] bringing also under his orders the sloops *Princess Royal* and *Northwest America*. The meeting with Martínez was very cordial, and Colnett might not have entered that port if the Spaniard had not met him with singular demonstrations of civility. Colnett, who a short while before did not dare to anchor out of respect for our colors, which he saw waving from the large rock that today serves as a fort, attempted, once inside, to execute the orders he had from Meares to establish himself in Nootka on the same land that Meares claimed to have purchased from Maquinna, and to enforce this attempt with arms if anyone tried to prevent him from carrying it out.

Although he found himself with inferior forces, Martínez of course had to oppose the demands which the Englishman haughtily set forth. The Spaniard them committed the indiscretion of insulting him, and even of putting his hand on his sword in order to kill him. It is likely that the churlish nature of each one precipitated things up to this point, since those who sailed with both complained of them equally and condemned their uncultivated boorishness.

Martínez ordered the arrest of his opponent and the seizure of all his ships. The Boston-men whom I have just named were witnesses to these acts.[7] The prisoners complained of having received cruel and inhuman treatment and having suffered the loss of various rather precious articles. The Spanish claimed to the contrary, and it is impossible to find impartial witnesses in order to extract the truth. It is certain that many of the English were

---

[5] The published version of *Noticias de Nutka* (p. 60) has the word *negociantes* (businessmen) whereas the several manuscripts read *navegantes*.

[6] Colnett arrived on July 3, 1789, after a ten-week voyage from Macao (Howay, ed., *Journal of Captain James Colnett*, p. 53).

[7] Joseph Ingraham (described by Bodega y Quadra as "an intelligent fellow of considerable talent and great experience on the coast") and Robert Gray.

able to go ashore, and that the first time they did so they complained to Maquinna and his relative Quelequem, weeping copiously, either from anger or from pain, about the insults and
violence inflicted by Martínez. They told the chiefs that [the
Spaniard] was a robber and had no other motive than his desire
to take the furs which they carried in their ships or to prevent
them from buying others from that time forward.

These chiefs, sympathizing with the unfortunate fate of their
friends and ignorant of the right which authorized the proceedings of Martínez, formed a dreadful concept of this official as a
ferocious pirate whose avarice did not respect a single thing.
Maquinna avoided seeing him more from dread than from indignation, since he did not have the courage to pass in front of
Martínez' frigate. Quelequem showed less cowardice and went to
visit Don Gonzalo [López] de Haro in the packet boat *San Carlos*.
In the wardroom he boldly protested Martínez' conduct and assured Haro that this would not be a motive for breaking the
friendship which he had cultivated with the other Spaniards.
Haro on his part tried to calm him, gave him various presents,
and sent him off well-satisfied. When [Quelequem] had returned
ashore, Martínez saw him from the quarterdeck of the *Princesa*
and urged him to come aboard, probably with the intention of
also giving him presents and removing the impression of the
slanderous report of the English. But the Indian did not con-
descend to accept the invitation because Martínez was a *pisec*,
that is, a wicked man, and had robbed his friends. He said that
neither Maquinna nor himself would be safe from his greed and
cruelty.

This was a small affront to cause this officer to have taken the
barbaric resolution of ordering [Quelequem] shot to death.[8] He

---

[8] Martínez recorded the event on July 13, 1789, as follows: "Irritated by
such slanderous (degrading) words, I took a rifle . . . and aiming it, I mis-
fired. One of my sailors who saw this took another and fired it, from which
shot Keleken [Quelequem] died. The unjust reasoning and improper proceedings of said Indian and the conversation which he had with Captain

should have respected in this prince those noble sentiments of friendship which he professed for the English, and which Martínez could have gained for himself and all the Spaniards by awaiting another occasion to undeceive him prudently and treat him more humanely. The body of Quelequem, which remained floating on the water, and the blood with which the sea was tinted, saddened the natives beyond measure. The Spaniards themselves, who even today still detest this murder, placed on the reputation of the pilot from San Blas the black mark of abomination with which he is generally regarded throughout the northern archipelago. The timid Maquinna abandoned his village and went for protection to that of Wickinanish in Clayoquot, leaving Martínez to establish his barracks on the land which he had abandoned.[9]

---

Colnett the morning of the 3rd . . . during which Colnett had said that he had become owner of the land and that he would throw us all out of this port, were put in their proper places (Martínez, *Diario*).

[9] Editor Barreiro-Meiro believes that Moziño felt a certain animosity toward Martínez because he was ignorant of all the facts and relied partially upon English information. "The bad reputation which Martínez has suffered even to this day was spread by England because it served her ends. But Mociño, before listening to this propaganda, should have examined all of the sources of that time and those in Mexico . . . which should have been abundant. . . . That Mociño did not know the diary of Martínez is easy to demonstrate. In his account, Mociño says that Quelequem was executed, and this is not certain. He also says that Maquinna and his subordinates retired from the village after the death of Quelequem and did not return to Nootka until the arrival of Bodega y Quadra's commission, of which Maquinna formed a part. If Mociño had read the diary, he would have learned that, after the incident, Maquinna had various interviews with Martínez . . . gave Martínez four otter skins . . . and promised that when the Spaniards abandoned Nootka, he [Maquinna] would take care of the great cross . . . the garden, and the cut timber." Barreiro-Meiro cites several other visits by Maquinna and neighboring Indians.

# ARTICLE NO. 10

*Arrival of Eliza and Alberni in 1790; their industry and reconciliation of Maquinna with the Spanish*

I N the following year of 1790, Lieutenant Don Francisco Eliza, accompanied by Don Pedro Alberni, captain of the Catalonian Volunteers, went to relieve the command.[1] To the industrious character of the latter, which in no way belies the general character of his province,[2] are owing the houses, offices, and gardens which have provided relief and comfort to many navigators.[3] Alberni guided his troops in the cultivation of the fields, excavated

[1] Francisco Eliza was among the naval officers (with Bodega y Quadra) who accompanied Viceroy Revilla Gigedo to Mexico in 1789. In addition to commanding the expedition to Nootka in 1790, Eliza undertook the exploration of the Strait of Juan de Fuca in 1791. According to Wagner (*Spanish Explorations in the Strait of Juan de Fuca*, p. 7), Eliza succeeded Bodega y Quadra as commandant of the Department of San Blas and was still attached to the department in 1803 with the rank of commander. Lieutenant Colonel Pedro de Alberni served three years in Cerro Prieto and seven years as commandant of Nayarit in New Spain before his assignment to Nootka in 1789. Alberni was commanding officer of the Primera Compañía Franca de Voluntarios de Cataluña from December, 1789, to September, 1792. Out of a company of eighty men, seventy-six accompanied Alberni to Nootka in 1790. The career of Eliza is found in "Antiguedades de los Oficiales de Guerra de la Armada," MN, MS 1161, and that of Alberni in AGI, Mexico 1446.

[2] The Yale MS clarifies this with the note, "The Principality of Catalonia."

[3] Menzies described Alberni's efforts in detail: ". . . there were also several spots fenced in, well cropped with the different European garden stuffs,

wells, constructed aqueducts, raised a quantity of poultry, and through his assiduous effort made all his crew capable of defending themselves from famine. Eliza, for his part, followed this example, and both officers employed all their wisdom in attracting the good will of the natives. With his rare insight, Alberni realized Maquinna's tendency to listen with appreciation to flattery, and in order to induce him to visit the Spanish, with whom he had broken all familiar communications since the tragic passing of Quelequem, he composed a verse, with the few words he then knew of the language, celebrating the greatness of Maquinna and the friendship which Spain professed for this chief and all his nation.

> *Macuina, Macuina, Macuina*
> *Asco Tais hua-cás;*
> *España, España, España*
> *Hua-cás Macuina Nutka.*

"Maquinna, Maquinna, Maquinna is a great prince and friend of ours; Spain, Spain, Spain is the friend of Maquinna and Nootka." He taught his troops to sing it to the tune of "El Marabú,"[4] so that the savages could hear it and tell it to their *tais*. The pleasant stratagem produced exactly the effect its author desired. Maquinna came at once and asked that they sing his eulogy several times over so that he could memorize it and repeat it, as I came to hear it after two years.

Two things in the conduct of our men during this time seem

---

which grew here very luxuriantly . . . & notwithstanding the advantage & great utility that were thus derived from Horticulture in this Country, it seems not one of the Natives had yet followed so laudable an example . . . " (Newcombe, ed., *Menzies' Journal*, p. 111).

[4] A popular Andalusian folk song of the eighteenth century still sung by Spanish sailors:

> *Tienes unos ojitos de pica porte*
> *con el ay! con el mara-bay*
> *con el u! con el mara-bu*
> *Ay! que me mu Ay! que me muero*
> *San Juan de la Cruz.*

reprehensible to me. The first was ordering that the Indians who came at night to steal some metal hoops from the casks and barrels should be fired upon, since they could have made restitution for this crime, and been warned that the next time they would suffer another penalty, but not that of death, which we ourselves do not inflict on our criminals for robberies of such little consideration. The second was the violence with which they seized lumber in the village of Tlu-pana-nutl to construct the principal building of our establishment. This *tais* had no other lumber than that used in his lodges, and it is an injustice as great as that of robbery to compel any man by force of arms to sell what he needs for himself and does not wish to give up for any price. Eliza's mistake in this episode was in not sending with the soldiers and sailors who carried out this attack some of his pilots, whose innate good nature would have served as a brake on those men who ordinarily become brutal and fierce when they are given a little authority.[5]

Despite these incidents, we found these officers [Alberni and Eliza] in the most perfect harmony with the *taises* and all the natives, and they confessed being in their debt for various benefits. Maquinna, noticing that Eliza's table lacked the viands he had observed in the beginning, and learning from this the low state of his food supply, ordered his *meschimes* to take him fish every day and to accept no payment for their gift. Moreover, since he knew that Eliza was accustomed to having meat, scarcely a week passed when he did not supply him with one or two deer. When Eliza appeared to be needier, Maquinna visited him with

---

[5] Curiously, John Hoskins of the *Columbia* recorded in his diary in June, 1791: "On my landing I gave positive orders to the boats crew, not to offer the least umbrage to the natives; and I verily believe they did not, though no doubt it is too often the case that sailors, when no officer is with them, from their ignorance of the language, either miscomprehend the natives, or the natives them; thus each deeming the other insulted, a quarrel ensues, and the officers who are on shore fall a sacrifice to it. [A]s well in civilized, so in savage governments, from small causes, great evils spring" (Howay, ed., *Voyages of the "Columbia,"* p. 192).

greater frequency and cordiality. Alberni received similar benefits from Tlu-pana-nutl, and almost everyone lived with the savages with the greatest familiarity.

I am a witness of the singular affection which they professed for the captain of the Volunteers [Alberni], even after they had lost hope of seeing him again. The Prince Nana-quius, especially, begged me to give him many embraces in his name and assure him that he loved him dearly. They are outstandingly grateful and will always remember their benefactors. The memory of Señores Malaspina[6] and Bustamante,[7] [Alcalá] Galiano and Valdés,[8] will be eternal in that nation for the friendly and generous manner in which they behaved during the short time they remained among its inhabitants.

Maquinna gave to Eliza the land of which Martínez had taken possession, on the condition that it be returned to him (as soon as the Spanish left), so that he could establish his village there, as had all of his ancestors and as he himself had done during the first years of his government.

[6] The Yale MS reads, " . . . Señores Malaspina (1) y Bustamante (2) Galeano (2) y Valdés (2)," with the corresponding notes: "(1) Chief of the Expedition of Corvettes which is found going around the world. (2) Naval Officers, his subordinates."

[7] José Bustamante y Guerra, in command of the *Atrevida*, accompanied Malaspina's *Descubierta* to the Northwest Coast and Nootka in 1791.

[8] Dionísio Alcalá Galiano and Cayetano Valdés, subordinate officers of the Malaspina expedition in 1791 who returned to Nootka during Moziño's visit in command of the schooners *Sutil* and *Mexicana*. As noted above, the Yale MS was probably adapted from *Noticias de Nutka* by Jose Cardero, artist and scribe of the Alcalá Galiano-Valdés visit of 1792.

# ARTICLE NO. II

*Representation of Meares to the Government of England against the Spanish; agreement of both nations; voyage to Nootka of Don [Juan] Francisco de la Bodega [y Quadra] in order to carry it out; commission given by the viceroy of Mexico to the author for the investigation of natural resources; sociability of the Nootkans; utility of the missions and of the promotion of agriculture*

As soon as Meares learned the unfortunate outcome of Colnett's expedition, without attempting beforehand to examine in the least the motives and circumstances of the arrest, he immediately presented a memorial against the Spanish nation in the House of Commons, exaggerating Martínez' unjust proceedings and the enormous losses his trade had suffered for this reason.[1] In order to give even more force to his presumptuous claims, Meares said that he had taken possession of that port in the name of His Britannic Majesty, having preceded this with a formal purchase, and that the Spanish pilot had violently taken possession of it and ruined the corresponding interests of various

[1] Meares, *Memorial.*

stockholders in the value of more than six hundred thousand pesos.[2]

[Meares] succeeded in inflaming his nation and stimulating preparations for war which were not carried out because of the agreement signed at San Lorenzo el Real in [17]91[3] by their Excellencies Señor Conde de Florida Blanca and Fitzherbert, plenipotentiaries of the two monarchies.[4] The ministers agreed between themselves that the Spanish would make restitution to the British subjects for the portions of land which the latter complained had been taken from them at Nootka and Clayoquot during the month of April, 1789, and would compensate them for all losses which they said they had suffered.[5]

To carry out this commission, the English government gave commensurate orders to Captain George Vancouver, who, a few months before, had left the Thames, in command of the frigate *Discovery* and brigantine *Chatham*. His purposes were to reconnoiter the Northwestern Coast of North America, examine the Strait of Juan de Fuca, and continue to survey the continent up to Cook Inlet[6] in order to solve finally the problem of the passage to the Atlantic Ocean [Northwest Passage].[7]

---

[2] Meares (*ibid.*, p. 88) shows the actual losses sustained by the "Associated Merchants of London and India" to be 153,433 Spanish dollars and probable losses at 500,000 Spanish dollars. The amount finally paid by Spain for damages was $210,000. See also Howay, ed., *Dixon-Meares Controversy*, pp. 4–15.

[3] The agreement was signed October 28, 1790.

[4] The Count of Florida Blanca, Spanish Secretary of State (1777–92), favored peace and the formation of an armed neutrality against England; Alleyne Fitzherbert (Baron St. Helens) was sent to Madrid in 1791 to settle the Nootka Sound Controversy. He was appointed ambassador to the Hague in 1794.

[5] The negotiations leading up to and full terms of the treaty, discussed on pp. xli–xlii, are found in Manning, "The Nootka Sound Controversy."

[6] The published version of the *Noticias* reads *Riá* de Cook whereas the Yale MS, Revilla Gigedo MS, and Museo Naval MSS have *Punta* de Cook.

[7] See George Vancouver, *A Voyage of Discovery to the North Pacific Ocean and Round the World* (3 vols; London: C. J. and J. Robinson; J. Edwards, 1798); Anderson, *Life and Voyages of George Vancouver*; and Meany, *Vancouver's Discovery of Puget Sound*.

On our part, Captain of the Royal Navy Don Juan Francisco de la Bodega y Quadra was commissioned to draw up, in consort with the English, a geographic chart [of the coast] from the aforementioned strait to the Port of San Francisco of New California.[8] To observe the various items that nature might present in these new discoveries, his Excellency, the Count of Revilla Gigedo, was pleased to confer upon me the honor of this commission, giving me as a companion Don Atanasio Echeverría, one of the best artists of our botanical expedition in New Spain.[9] With his help and that of Don Joseph María Maldonado, second surgeon of the Royal Navy and formerly chief naturalist of this same expedition, I was able to gather more than two hundred species of plants and various animals which I will add to the investigations of this kind on which I am now working.[10]

We actually arrived on that island [Nootka] on April 29, 1792, and at that moment began the friendship and good feeling between ourselves and the natives. Never during all the time of our long residence did they give us the slightest reason for displeasure.

Almost as soon as we anchored, Maquinna came to welcome the Spanish commandant, referring to the harmonious relationship Eliza had preserved with him. He still detested the memory of that officer who had killed Quelequem and offered to pay any price for his [Martínez'] gun, in case we might have it. Maquin-

---

[8] Bodega y Quadra described the purpose of his commission at Nootka in 1792 as follows: "The sovereigns of Spain and England, not satisfied of the truth of the events which have occurred in places so far from Europe; and enheartened by a sincere desire to end the subsequent differences, have agreed to leave the examination to the direction of two commissioners from both Courts. With this objective and that of coordinating a general chart in order to propose the boundaries, I anchored in this port the 29th of April . . . " ("Viaje de 1792").

[9] "Orden del Virrey," Mexico, December 21, 1791, AGN, Historia 527.

[10] "Catálogo de los Animales y Plantas" (Appendix B); Moziño was referring to the work of the Royal Scientific Expedition of New Spain in gathering and classifying the plant species north of Mexico City. See Plates 19, 20, 21, 22, and 23.

na was received with the greatest appreciation and civility on the part of all, and he took his leave fully satisfied because of this and because of the gifts we presented not only to him but also to the *catlatis* [brothers of the chief] who accompanied him. Beginning the next day we saw our ships surrounded with canoes, and the islanders, filled with happiness, were ready to conduct our sailors to the shore for nothing more than the small token of a piece of bread.

It causes me inexpressible wonder to hear various bitter criticisms of the reputation of these natives, when not one example can be cited which could ever serve as proof of their perversity. During the five months that we were living among them, we did not experience one offense on their part. They filled the house of the commandant day and night. Maquinna slept in his bedroom; Quio-comasia and Nana-quius did the same in mine. There were many times when more than fifty remained in the living room. The occasions on which some small thefts were noticed were very few, although there were at hand several articles that would have been very convenient for them to possess. Many of our officers went alone and without arms to visit a number of villages, conducted in the savages' own canoes. They always returned impressed by the affection and gentleness they had observed in everyone.

What a pity that they could not in general say the same about us. The sailors, either as a result of their almost brutal upbringing or because they envied the humane treatment the commandant and other officers always gave the natives, insulted them at various times, crippled some and wounded others, and did not fail to kill several. Humanity is the greatest characteristic of civilization. All the sciences and arts have no value if they serve only to make us cruel and haughty.

Several of the natives, especially Nana-quius, Nat-zape,[11]

[11] The Yale MS includes Nat-zape, whose name is omitted in the published version.

Quio-comasia, and Tata-no, learned to speak quite a bit of our language. The facility with which they grasped most of the things we wanted to explain to them should make us very sorry that the ministers of the Gospel have not taken advantage of such a fine opportunity to plant the Catholic faith among them. I know that the cross-bearers [priests][12] reported that a mission could not be established here because there was a lack of land that could be cultivated. What a small obstacle! As if a mission and improved land were synonymous! And could not a doctrine that was taught by fishermen in the first place be communicated to those who out of necessity, ignorance, and a lack of resources follow this profession? What results might have been achieved in four years, had the Spanish not abandoned Nootka or been without a chaplain! That is to say that if they had handled the savages with a little prudence and charity, they would now all be Christians, since they could not contradict the truths[13] [of the church] by either the proud philosophy of the Greeks or the superstition and power of the Romans.

Along with instruction in the principles of the true religion, they could have inspired the Indians with other ideas, whose execution brings well-known advantages to society. Agriculture could have been promoted not by trying to find actual farmland on the beach, or land that would be fertile without any work, but by exploring the interior of the island, clearing a large part of it, and cultivating those things that would be most appropriate to the soil. After so much time, working only little by little, the brush that today makes the mountains inaccessible should have been destroyed, and experiments conducted which would show positively whether or not our crops could be adapted to those parts.

If an area suitable for plantings were lacking here [at Nootka],

[12] The Yale MS adds a note that these priests were from the "College of Apostolic Missionaries of the Order of San Francisco in the City of Querétaro."
[13] The Yale MS reads, "the revealed truths."

[ 85 ]

one without disadvantages could surely be found on the Island of Quadra and Vancouver, which is larger and has a more benign climate because it is situated at a lower latitude. What the travelers say about the inclemency of American lands, compared with European ones of the same latitude, is confirmed by the experience, which should be understood, on the East Coast of this continent, where, nevertheless, the continuing efforts of the European colonists have been prosperous.

The summer, without doubt, is the best season in Nootka. If the inhabitants would make their plantings on the slopes of the hillsides, the frequent rains would not drown the roots with the rapid downpour of water, nor would the winds scatter the seeds because of the shelter they would have there. But let us return to our narrative.

# ARTICLE NO. 12

*Arrival of the English Commandant Vancouver; verification of the falsity of Meares's complaints; suspension of the agreement between the Spanish and the English commandants, who sent back their decision to their governments; reflections upon the usefulness of maintaining or abandoning the establishment, and method by which the Spanish could extend the fur trade*

C APTAIN Vancouver, who had entered to explore the Strait of Juan de Fuca at the beginning of April [1792], did not arrive until the end of August. At the outlet of the strait in 51° North latitude, Vancouver received the first news of the commission that awaited him, and of the provisions brought for his ships in the merchant vessel *Daedalus*.[1] Sr. [Bodega y] Quadra had not lost the opportunity to clarify the justice of the English

---

[1] The English brig *Venus*, sailing out of Nootka, encountered Vancouver on August 17, 1792, to give him a letter from Thomas News, commander of the *Daedalus*, and a message from Bodega y Quadra. The Spanish commandant wrote in his diary that "through Robert Gray . . . I knew that Vancouver had been inside the Strait since April and that he would surely leave it at 51°, where there was an inlet which connected with the Nuchimanes . . ."(Bodega y Quadra, "Viaje de 1792").

demands for restitution nor to ascertain the truth of the losses which Meares's trade had suffered.[2]

Since Meares bases his principal action upon the purchase he made from Maquinna, and the *tais* consistently denies such a purchase, affirming on the other hand, without pressure or persuasion, that Kendrick was the only one to whom he had sold a piece of land at Maquinnas; and since he also affirms that Eliza and [Bodega y] Quadra were those to whom he had given another piece of land in Yuquatl, I believe that the English themselves should recognize the falsity with which the complainant, whom Maquinna calls "*Aita-Aita* Meares" ("Liar Meares"), proceeded.[3]

No less absurd are the benefits Meares claims to have derived from his commerce, since by merely reading the reports of many others following the same trade at that time one can easily verify the deep slump which the price of sea otter skins had taken. Those of the best quality could scarcely be sold for forty-five pesos, yet even so Meares charged the Spanish one hundred for each one. These are a luxury article for the Chinese, who pay for them in proportion to their scarcity, and since they were filling the warehouses of Canton, they had been losing value annually. Even Colnett himself had the misfortune of not being able to sell one skin in Asia and of finding himself obligated to carry them on to London, according to what Captain Robert Broughton has told me several times.[4]

By virtue of all this and in accordance with the instructions our commandant had received, he offered the English commissioner the possession and ownership of the land on which Meares had built his hut, at the same time permitting them to use that which

---

[2] Bodega y Quadra's journal contains copies of the numerous letters and declarations made by Gray, Ingraham, Viana, Maquinna, and others, regarding the events of 1789. See also Manning, "The Nootka Sound Controversy."

[3] See Article 11.

[4] Lieutenant William Robert Broughton, commander of the *Chatham* on Vancouver's expedition.

Maquinna had given to the Spanish and which they had cultivated with prodigious labor.

But the Englishman was never willing to reconcile himself to
partial possession. He always insisted upon demanding, in the
name of his monarch, sovereignty over all that land and free access to the rest of the coast down to ten leagues north of San
Francisco. The latter did not really enter the controversy, because
that decision was in the recent agreement;[5] but the former [sov-
ereignty over Nootka] certainly exceeded the expressed powers
of the Spanish commandant. He was therefore unable to carry out
the agreement and resolved to suspend it until the courts of
Madrid and London reached a new decision based upon the reports which their respective commissioners would make with
appropriate ingenuity.[6]

The English commandant was no less humane toward the Indians than the Spanish had been. Both left an example of goodness among them. "*Cococoa* [like] Quadra," they say, "*Cococoa*
Vancouver," when they want to praise the good treatment of any
of the captains who command the other ships. May God grant
that they may never be dealt with except by men about whom
they can say the same, and may this fine example have thousands
of imitators from this time forward.[7]

---

[5] The Nootka Convention of October 28, 1790.

[6] Vancouver and Bodega y Quadra got along very well personally, and the
British were duly impressed by the treatment they received. Menzies wrote,
"Don Quadra whose benevolent mind seemed wholly occupied in con-
tributing to our entertainments & amusements, now proposed . . . to take
a jaunt up the Sound . . . " (Newcombe, ed., *Menzies' Journal*, p. 115), and
Vancouver himself described "a dinner of five courses, consisting of a
superfluity of the best provisions," elegantly served to them upon their
arrival, and noted that the "politeness, hospitality, and friendship shewn
on all occasions by Señor Quadra, induced Mr. Broughton and myself, with
several of the officers and gentlmen of both vessels, to dine at his table
almost every day . . . " (quoted in Meany, *Vancouver's Discovery of Puget
Sound*, pp. 303, 314).

[7] Vancouver wrote in his journal, "I could not help observing with a
mixture of surprise and pleasure, how much the Spaniards had succeeded
in gaining the good opinion and confidence of these people [the Nootka In-

Assuming that the English, as it seems from the facts to which we have referred, did not have any right to claim the possession which they demanded, and that the Spanish had proven their right legally in the terms authorized by public law, it becomes a political problem, the solution of which does not lack supporters on either side. Is it convenient for Europe [Spain][8] to maintain that establishment, or on the contrary would it be more beneficial to her interests to abandon it?[9]

Forgive me for the boldness of frankly expressing my opinion about a situation which other persons have considered in a very

---

dians] . . ." (Meany, *Vancouver's Discovery of Puget Sound*, p. 304). The friendship of the Nootka Indians was enjoyed during the entire period of Spanish occupation and indeed taken for granted by all visitors to the Northwest Coast until tragedy struck in March, 1803. As the result of real or imagined insults from Captain John Salter of the *Boston*, Maquinna led a surprise attack and his Indians killed and decapitated all but two of the twenty-seven men on board. John Jewitt, a young blacksmith of Hull, England, and sailmaker John Thompson of Philadelphia were captured and held for two and one-half years as slaves. Young Jewitt kept a diary of his experiences from which he published his subsequent account of Nootka and its inhabitants. (See Brown, ed., *The Adventures of John Jewitt*.)

[8] Although the Spanish word is "Europa," Moziño undoubtedly meant "España. An error was probably made in copying.

[9] The Yale MS substitutes the following in place of the two preceding paragraphs of the published version of *Noticias de Nutka*: "Both cabinets have already agreed on this point, the Spanish ceding to the English the sovereign possession of Nootka, which act of delivery and receipt was effected at the beginning of January, 1795 [*sic*], by the Brigadier [General] of the Army Don José de Alava and by Mr. Thomas Pierce, Lieutenant of the Royal Marines of England. It [now] becomes a political problem, the solution of which does not lack supporters for either side. Was it convenient for Spain to preserve that establishment? Or, on the contrary, did its cession result in any benefits to its interests?" The writer is referring to the final Nootka treaty signed at Madrid on January 11, 1794, the provisions of which were to be carried out again by Bodega y Quadra and Vancouver. The former died in March, 1794, and was replaced by General Alava as commandant of San Blas and Nootka commissioner. Vancouver and Alava met briefly at Nootka Sound in September, 1794; since the Spanish commissioner was without official instructions, nothing was accomplished and Vancouver sailed for home. His replacement, Lieutenant Pierce, sailed with the *Activo* from San Blas on January 13, 1795, met Alava in Monterey, and the two commissioners proceeded to Nootka on March 1. The final ceremony and abandonment took place on March 23, 1795.

different manner, and for which I perhaps lack the indispensable knowledge of the various views which the governments may have.

Up to now this establishment has not produced any advantage in favor of the crown, but, on the contrary, the enormous expenses it has had to pay out are notorious. Even private individuals have achieved nothing more than a miserable trade in furs, and the hopes of making it absolutely lucrative, besides being extremely remote, could be realized just as well, as the Boston-men have done and are still doing, if the port were independent. Nootka is a place where one finds very few furs, and these come from the Nuchimanes, Clayoquot, and Tutusi. The great collections are made on Prince William, the [Queen] Charlotte [Islands], and the Strait of [Juan de] Fuca. The second place is occupied by the Clayoquot, and Nootka attracts foreigners at present only because they can supply themselves with water and firewood at no risk.

The security of our possessions in New Spain and California is neither insured more nor endangered less by our being owners of this island, since if our enemies should seek to establish a site next to our territories, in order to invade us with greater facility, there is a distance of two hundred leagues between Nootka and San Francisco which is left free for them. There are various coves such as Gray's Harbor, Ensenada de los Mártires,[10] Entrada de Heceta [Columbia River], Sidman,[11] la Bodega [Tomales Bay], and so forth in which to protect a considerable number of ships.

[10] The mouth of the Hoh River in Washington where some of Captain William Barkley's men were killed in 1787. It is sometimes confused with Punta de Martires (Point Grenville, Washington) where Bodega y Quadra, in command of the *Sonora* with the Heceta expedition in July, 1775, saw seven of his crew members killed by hostile Indians.

[11] Henry R. Wagner in *The Last Spanish Exploration of the Northwest Coast and the Attempt to Colonize Bodega Bay* (San Francisco, 1931), p. 18, says the port was named by Captain James Baker of the *Jenny* after the ship's owner, Sidenham Teast of Bristol. Baker gave the name to a port at the mouth of a small river (probably the Umpqua) at 43° 40', where he had spent ten or twelve days trading in 1791.

Furthermore I consider they would gain a better post on any one of the Sandwich Islands, where they could supply themselves with local provisions without difficulty and where many Europeans could establish themselves. More than fifteen years have passed since those islands were discovered, and the English have still not planned to establish a colony on them which would in time indemnify them for the loss of those that fought for independence in the northeast of this continent.

The discovery of Tahiti and the Friendly Island group made us suspect not many years ago that the English had some tentative designs on Peru. For this reason Tahiti was occupied by us, but was relinquished at the end of two years despite the abundance of various articles which nature had supplied and the great probability of obtaining others by industry.[12] Afterward the English came there on repeated occasions because it was an excellent port of call for their voyages, and time has convinced us that there is no danger that could threaten us in this area. If my observations do not deceive me too much, England's intentions are directed principally toward extending and invigorating her commerce. Consequently she would expose herself to ruin if she should try to multiply her colonies without taking into consideration that

[12] Captain Domingo Bonaechea, commander of an expedition of discovery and exploration to Tahiti and neighboring islands in the frigate *Aquila* in 1772, returned to Tahiti two years later, accompanied by the packet boat *Jupiter*, under order of Viceroy Manuel de Amat of Peru. Bonaechea was commissioned to establish a Spanish settlement in the name of Carlos III, found a mission for Christianizing the natives, and explore the neighboring islands. The captain of the *Jupiter*, José de Andía y Varela, kept a journal of the expedition in the true scientific tradition of the period, noting the geography, natural resources, fauna and flora, customs, and language of the natives. Bonaechea died in 1774 before returning to Peru; the mission established in Tahiti failed and was abandoned the following year. See José de Andía y Varela, *Relación del viaje hecho a la isla de Amat, por otro nombre Otahiti . . . en los años 1774 y 1775*, edited by Joaquin de Sarriera (Barcelona: J. Porter, 1947), and Bolton Glanville Corney, *The Quest and Occupation of Tahiti by Emissaries of Spain, 1772–1776* (London: Printed for the Hakluyt Society, 1913).

the more land she occupied, the more scattered would be her subjects, who, united, have the power of the entire nation.

The present circumstances do not permit us to fortify Nootka in such a way that it could in any eventuality put up a vigorous resistance that would compel respect for our flag. For this purpose at least a battalion would be necessary, and it can be seen that its maintenance, if one recalls the mounting costs for the frigate [*Santa*] *Gertrudis* alone after a very few months, would reach nearly one million [pesos] in each of the first three or four years that would have to be invested in clearing the land and preparing it for cultivation, the result of which should be evident from what I have said before. Meanwhile it is generally necessary to bring all provisions from San Blas. Added to this are the expenses necessary for supply ships, and those which are indispensable to maintain control of the bay, since there are more than fifty English ships of various types, armed for war, which cruise through that sea.

In addition to all this, it would be impossible to cut off the commerce engaged in by the foreigners with the natives. They can anchor in Esperanza Inlet, at Nuchimanes, and even come up to Maquinnas without our artillery being capable of hindering them. But suppose we fortified all these entrances in such a manner that no one could approach them without our permission? Could this be done with Queen Charlotte Island, from which it is possible to go to California with the same or greater facility, and in the same number of days, as from Nootka? And what would we do with Bucareli Inlet? And farther to the south would not Clayoquot, the Archipelago de Carrasco [Barkley Sound], and others remain unguarded?

Anyone can see that six or eight thousand men would scarcely be enough to guard these points, and that, even if we took exclusive possession of the fur trade, it probably would not defray the enormous expenses which our defense would require.

The first object of our attentions should be California. There our conquest has taken roots, our religion has been propagated, and our hopes are greatest for obtaining obvious advantages to benefit all the monarchy. The Port of San Francisco (let the pilots of San Blas say what they wish) is the best of any that have been seen on the entire coast, according to the testimony of the celebrated navigator Vancouver, who was greatly surprised by the bad reports of it that were given to him in Nootka.

The Bay of Monterey is very large and dangerous only during the winter, and the same could be said of San Diego and the Santa Barbara Channel.

Throughout most of New California, the landscape is very beautiful, the soil fertile, the mountains wooded, and the climate benign. There is no European product that could not be successfully grown there. There is pasturage for all kinds of livestock. These have multiplied so prodigiously that between the Presidio of Monterey and the Mission of Carmel are counted more than ten thousand head of cattle and a considerable number of horses and sheep. In the sea that bathes its coasts, fish swarm and whales, sea otters, and sea lions abound. In short, God is generously offering an immensity of wealth which we are not enjoying for lack of people. Five hundred leagues of territory do not have as inhabitants even two thousand persons who can be regarded as vassals of our monarchy, and of these not even five hundred, including women and children, can be called civilized people [*gente de razón*].[13]

The garrison of San Francisco is composed of only fifteen soldiers, and that of Monterey scarcely exceeds thirty. The same is true of San Diego and the [Santa Barbara] Channel, respec-

[13] The Yale MS includes the note, "By this term are distinguished those in New Spain who are not Indians, although they might be Mulattos, etc." The total population of "civilized people" in California as of 1790 was 583 men and 382 women; number of livestock, agricultural population, and detailed population statistics are given in Cutter, *Malaspina in California*, Appendix D, pp. 82–83.

tively. There is no presidio that includes a battery of guns, and, even if there was one, it would be useless because they are all unskilled in the handling of cannon.

In no other place could our enemies establish themselves more advantageously, and consequently none demands more the attention of our diligent government. Dividing our forces into small garrisons weakens us more and more. Not only Nootka, but all those posts of the north ought to be also abandoned to protect California and promote there the branches of industry for which it is suitable; so that far from being a liability to the state, as it has been until now, it could sustain itself and contribute to the needs of the Crown.

One of the quickest means to achieve this end would be the fur trade, which, if taken up with diligence by the Spanish, should belong to them exclusively within a very few years. We have, in our possessions, all the items that circulate in this trade; abundant copper in Michoacán; many textiles in Querétaro, Cholula, and other places; crude hats throughout the kingdom; abalone shells in Monterey; and so forth. Navigation ought to be less costly for us and closer to the port of departure and points of arrival. We have an abundance of foodstuffs which can be obtained from the Californias and the facility to purchase these easily. We can therefore pay more to the Indians for the furs and sell them to the Chinese more cheaply.

Anyone who wishes to follow prudently a business of this kind, according to my opinion and that of various informed persons with whom I have discussed this matter, should embark from Acapulco for Manila with as much copper, cloth, blankets, and so forth, as he can carry. From there he should go to Macao[14] to procure cheaply a ship for which he would expend a large amount of capital if he had it constructed in the shipyard of San Blas. The enormous sums which the King has invested in the shipyard of this department [of San Blas] and the low price of

14 The Yale MS adds "or Canton."

[ 95 ]

these vessels even in Manila itself are well known. Captain Ingraham's brigantine *Hope* has a greater capacity in the hold and more comfortable cabin and sleeping quarters than our *Activo;* ours is a round and deep ship, his has a raised wasteboard and an excellent deck. The *Hope* has rounded Cape Horn with very strong winds, something which ours perhaps could not do without some repairs which our commandant is planning. The Boston ship is mounted with excellent artillery, double canvas, and hemp rigging. With all these advantages it is valued at not more than three thousand pesos, and the *Activo* costs more than twenty-four thousand.

A Chinese crew earns less than one from San Blas, and consequently should be preferred to the latter; meanwhile a great number of idle people in our kingdom are applying themselves to sailing, placing themselves in a position good for the economy.

Immediately upon leaving Asia, it would seem advisable to turn one's prow to the north after having passed the Archipelago of San Lázaro, and to continue seeking land, by sailing rather close to it, especially from Cook Inlet, so as not to lose sight of the various inlets, in most of which the English begin their trade. Nootka is an excellent port in which to supply oneself with water and firewood, and one could perhaps succeed in buying some pelts here. Various navigators have told me that, following the route I have indicated, one should be in this port at the end of three months even when contrary winds have caused some delay.

At the entrance of [Juan de] Fuca, after having stopped at Clayoquot and Carrasco, one will have completed the major collection of the most excellent sea otters in exchange for the items that have been taken out of New Spain.

If one brings some merchandise from Asia, one can trade these for skins from California, whose ports should all be visited for the purpose of carrying on trade. Here ships can be replenished with fresh provisions and can set sail directly for San Blas again to obtain the copper and so forth for the trading of the following season. One active trader can make at least two trips every three years and realize a minimum of 300 percent on each one of them despite the reduction which the initial price of sea otters has suffered and the frequent restrictions of the emperor of China.

The exportation of grain and livestock will make agriculture flourish in New California, and the exportation of copper and cloth will multiply the looms of New Spain and promote the shipping industry. This is already an advantage in favor of the nation, and from it will result another very large one if, in order to obtain merchandise from China, it does not have to pay out its silver and can obtain everything the Manila galleon[15] carries in exchange for sea otters.

As the Spanish traders along the coast increase in number, necessity itself will make the English and other foreigners retire. In this way, by reaping benefits instead of incurring expenses, we will succeed in securing our possessions and bringing about happiness and prosperity.

---

[15] The annual galleon from the Orient was called the *"Nao de Philipinas"* or *"Nao de China."*

# Appendix A

*Brief Dictionary of the Terms That Could Be Learned
of the Language of the Natives of Nootka*

| Dios | God | Coa-utz, Qua-utz |
| El Príncipe del Infierno | Prince of Hell | Iz-mitz |
| El Cielo | Heaven | Nas, Naz |
| El Infierno | Hell | Pinapula |
| El Alma | Soul | Coatzma |
| El Entendimiento | Intellect | Tli-mas-tec-nec |
| El Cuerpo | Body | O-u-matle |
| Cabeza | Head | Tagetcite, Tag-chite, Toscite |
| Cabello | Hair | Api-si-up |
| Coronilla | Crown | Apet-tzatque |
| Nuca | Nape of the neck | Indenix-taez, Yndeniat-zatz |
| Frente | Forehead | Ap-pe-a |
| Cexas | Eyebrows | A-ci-chi, Acac-ci-chi |
| Pestañas | Eyelashes | Achap-psim, Achag-psimg |
| Ojos | Eyes | Caa-hsi |
| Orbita del ojo | Eye socket | Oahtl-oahtl |
| Nariz | Nose | Nit-za, Nip-za |
| Labios | Lips | Chipitl-esma |
| Boca | Mouth | Ictal-tzutl, Ietla-tzutl |
| Dientes | Teeth | Chichi-chi, Chicohi |

| | | |
|---|---|---|
| Lengua | Tongue | Chup |
| Paladar | Palate | Apeza-meza |
| Ubula o campanilla | Uvula, staphyle | Cachi-yu-me, Chachi-yu-me |
| Ventanas de la nariz | Nostrils | Cus-cu-tla-temá, Cus-cu-tlate |
| Mandíbulas | Mandibles, jawbone | Tzi-huap |
| Carrillos | Cheeks | Ha-a-mas |
| Orejas | Ears | Pa-pé |
| Conducto auditibo | Auditory canal | Cocu-himé-himé, Cuachimé-himé |
| Barba, bigote y bozo | Beard, mustache and beard | Apac-chimé |
| Barba | | Apa-tzutl, Apopsima |
| Hombros | Shoulders | Tlaha-pimitl |
| Espaldas | Back | Inapatl |
| Espinas | Spine | Co-o-nez |
| Pecho | Chest | Tlapetz-ahuma |
| Tetas | Breasts | Eni-ma |
| Costillas | Ribs | Natlah-caz-te, Natlag-caz-te |
| Escrobíluca | Chest cavity | Ih-ni-yutl |
| Estómago | Stomach | Tije-hue-né, Tat-chá |
| Vientre | Abdomen | Ic-tac-tlas |
| Ombligo | Navel | Ai-me-né |
| Asentaderas | Buttocks | Y-tac-tle |
| El Corazón | Heart | Tug-tu-ja |
| Intestinos | Intestine | Tzi-yup |
| Vegiga de la orina | Urinary bladder | Az-pa-tu |
| Utero | Uterus | Tanat-zas |
| Brazo | Arm | Ca-ya-pta |
| Sobaco | Armpit | A-a-pa-zuntl |
| Escápulas | Shoulder blade | Tlah-tza-pe |
| Mano | Hand | Cucu-nic-zu, Cu-cumit-zu |
| Dedos | Fingers | Uc-tza |
| Pulgar | Thumb | Ehja-comitz |
| Indice | Index finger | Copeh-yac |
| Medio | Middle finger | Ta-yec |
| Anular | Ring finger | O-at-zo |

| | | |
|---|---|---|
| Meñique | Little finger | Cahtl-ac |
| Quadrilles | Haunchbones | Apezuh-tatchi, Apezuh-thtle |
| Rodilla | Knee | Chah-tzu-te |
| Espinilla | Shinbone | A-ama-nutl |
| Pantorrilla | Calf of the leg | Ta-nua |
| Tobillo | Ankle | Azh-xi |
| Pie | Foot | Tlis-tlen |
| Planta del pie | Sole of the foot | Apat-zutl |
| Cutis | Skin | Tug-coac |
| Saliva | Saliva | Tatl-metz |
| Mocos | Mucous | Ante-mitz |
| Sudor | Perspiration | Tloptze-machitl |
| Orina | Urine | Oc-xitl |
| Escretos | Excrement | Tzu-mag |
| Leche | Milk | Clit-zitl |
| Sangre menstrua | Menstrual blood | Ait-tzat-tri |
| Loquivos | Afterbirth | Tzahuatz-cui |
| Podre | Pus | Tza-ca-mitz |
| Hombre | Man | Cha-cups |
| Mujer | Woman | Clutz-ma |
| Niño | Child (male) | Maetl-catzis |
| Niña | Child (female) | Chu-tzas |
| Muchacho | Boy | Ta-naz |
| Joven | Youth | Ahui-jletl |
| Mujer joven | Young woman | Ag-coatl |
| Viejo | Old man | Mig-tug |
| Decrépito | Decrepit | Ig-cheme |
| Doncella | Governess, maiden | Huiguite-txate, Otiquit |
| Preñada | Pregnant | Tlitl-tzitl |
| Parida | Birth | Tza-hautz-coc |
| Gemelos | Twins | Coa-yas |
| Padre | Father | Nu-hec-zo, Nu-huc-zó |
| Madre | Mother | U-mec-zo |
| Hijo | Son | Ta-na |
| Hermano | Brother | Ca-tla-ti |
| Hermana | Sister | Clutz-mup |
| Abuelo | Grandfather | Coa-uteh |
| Nieto | Grandson | Na-ec-zo |

| | | |
|---|---|---|
| Tio | Uncle | Cui-uteh |
| Sobrino | Nephew | Hu-e-o |
| Sobrina | Niece | At-ectzo, Atz-ec-zó |
| Suegro | Father-in-law | Co-ec-zó |
| Suegra | Mother-in-law | Co-ec-zo-duzma |
| Yerno | Son-in-law | Co-ec-zo |
| Nuera | Daughter-in-law | Co-ec-zo |
| Cuñado | Brother-in-law | In-mec-zo, Yu-mec-zo |
| Cuñada | Sister-in-law | Chinap-zec-zo |
| Hombre gibo | Hunch-back | Yeh-jumil |
| Hombre tuerto | One-eyed man | Pipe-zul |
| Hombre ciego | Blind man | Maco-ulg |
| Hombre bizco | Cross-eyed man | Ani-cha |
| Hombre con nube en el ojo | Man with something in his eye | Mumuc-zemé |
| Hombre sordo | Deaf man | U-pulg |
| Hombre cojo | Lame man (with a limp) | Quitzac-tle |
| Hombre tullido | Crippled man | U-pe-mitl |
| Hombre manco | One-armed, one-handed man | Coa-coat-zo |
| Hombre mudo | Dumb man | Mu-co-itl |
| Hombre alto de cuerpo | Abnormally tall man | Ig-e-pit |
| Hombre enano | Dwarf | Na-huat-zitl, Nagua-zitl |
| Hombre alegre | Happy man | Ap-fei, ap-jei |
| Hombre serio o enojado | Serious or angry man | Hui-jei, hui-gei |
| Hombre veraz | Truthful man | Tag-cotl |
| Hombre embustero | Liar | Aita-aita |
| Casa | House | Na-ja-ti, Ma-ja-ti |
| Pabimento | Floor | Iz-te-itl |
| Texado | Roof | Tlu-uc |
| Murallas | Walls | Tehit-te-ma |
| Rincones | Corners | Ame-ni-cuitl |
| Puerta | Door | Ta-xi |
| Ventanas | Windows | Naj-as |

| | | |
|---|---|---|
| Estera | Sleeping mat | Tle-jatl |
| Caxa | Box | Toco-nec |
| Sombrero | Hat | Tzia-pugs |
| Telas de las capas | Material for capes | Atyl-mopt |
| Esclavina | Cape | Cliti-ni-que |
| Cama | Bed | Chimi-ith, chimi-elg |
| Almohada | Pillow | Achuco-ini-me |
| Canoa | Canoe | Cha-patz |
| Sus barcos | Its seats | Ja-pa-nic |
| Remos o Canaletes | Oars or paddles | U-jua-pe |
| Red de pescar | Fishnet | Hua-hua-mitic |
| Serrucho | Handsaw | Tchu-juc |
| Fierró | Iron | Chi-qui-mi-ni |
| Cobre | Copper | Chi-pugs |
| Almagre | Red ochre | Cua-ja-mitz |
| Abalorio | Glass beading | Ato-jui, Tu-xui |
| Concha del Haliotis | Abalone shell | Iz-to-coti |
| Arco | Bow, arch | Mutz-ta-ti |
| Flecha | Arrow | Si-ja-ti |
| Peine | Comb | Tza-chi-cas |
| Nutria de Mar | Sea otter | Co-cotl |
| su piel | Its fur | Coa-tlac, quotlac |
| Oso | Bear | Chi-mitz, chi-mes |
| su piel | Its fur | Clit-jac, clitac |
| Venado | Deer | Mo-huec |
| Ardilla | Squirrel | Chatu-mitz |
| Raton | Rat | Ipz-co-ne |
| Perro | Dog | Ae-nitl, ae-mitz, anniel |
| Lobo marino | Seal | Cocoa-quitza |
| Cuero de zorro | Fox skin | Coyac-tutz, co-yac-tzac, coyac-quitza |
| Aguila | Eagle | Ahua-te-ne |
| Cuerbo comun | Common crow, large crow | Coo-xi-ne |
| Cuerbo glandario | Small crow | Ca-e-ne |
| Ansar | Goose | Ma-matl |
| Gabiota | Seagull | Co-ne |

| | | |
|---|---|---|
| Gorrion | Sparrow | Quitl-chup |
| Cuello | Neck | Eme-u-nitl |
| Pico | Beak | Tlup-cuman |
| Uñas | Claws | Niqui-yac |
| Alas | Wings | Tlabas-paa-to |
| Plumas de ellas | Their feathers | A-apsu-enetl |
| Cola | Tail | Naa-cha |
| Pescado | Fish | Su-ma |
| Ballena | Whale | Ma-ac |
| Salmón | Salmon | Tzu-ja |
| Arenque | Herring | Clutz-mit |
| Mojarra | Sea fish | Chitza-pa |
| Sardina | Sardine | Ami-multz |
| Pulpo | Octopus | Til-sup |
| Arbol | Tree | Su-chatz |
| Yerba | Grass | Mucu-metz |
| Raiz | Root | Mulg-me-metz |
| Tronco | Trunk | Suchas-te-me |
| Ramas | Branches | Tla-cai-teme |
| [H]ojas | Leaves | Tla-tla-caj-tre-me |
| Flor | Flower | Co-i-matz |
| Fruto | Fruit | Pat-ai-hua |
| Fruta en general | Fruit in general | Cha-mas |
| Pedazo de madera | Piece of wood | Tza-hu-mitz |
| Cielo | Sky | Nas |
| Sol | Sun | Upel |
| Luna | Moon | Ata-jaz |
| Estrellas | Stars | Taa-tuz |
| Nubes | Clouds | Silg-huaja-mitz |
| Relampago | Lightning | Tleg-chitl |
| Rayo | Ray, thunderbolt | Tug-ta |
| Lluvia | Rain | Mic-tla |
| Arco Iris | Rainbow | Chami-ehtl |
| Tierra | Land | Tzi-tzi-mitz |
| Montañas | Mountains | Nug-chi |
| Piedras | Rocks | Muc-zi-e |
| Arena | Sand | Muc-cu-metz |
| Agua | Water | Cha-ac |
| Nieve | Snow | Co-iz |
| Granizo | Hail | Cat-zumen |

| | | |
|---|---|---|
| [H]ielo | Ice | Coitz-coe, coug |
| Laguna | Lagoon | A-oc |
| Rio | River | Tza-ac |
| Mar | Ocean, sea | Tug-pel |
| Mar bonancible | Calm sea | Au-pac |
| Mar borrascoso | Stormy sea | Piseg-chist |
| Olas | Waves | Cuaug-cuaja |
| Fluxo | Flood tide | Ta-yutl |
| Refluxo | Ebb tide | Tzautl |
| Aire | Air, wind | Yue |
| Buen viento | Fair wind | Oco-maja |
| Viento duro | Heavy wind | Pishec-as-yue |
| Norte | North wind | Yu-ilx |
| Norueste | Northwest wind | A-chi-litl |
| Sur | South wind | Tu-chi |
| Fuego | Fire | E-nic, Inic |
| Llama | Flame | Ix-cuitz |
| Humo | Smoke | Coixt-coe |
| Ceniza | Ash | Tling-te-me |
| Calor | Heat | Tlug-pa |
| Frio | Cold | Ate-quit-zi-majas |
| Año | Year | Jachinic-xitle |
| Mes | Month | U-pel |
| Dia | Day | Nas-chitl |
| Dia de Verano | Summer day | Yac-nas |
| Dio de Invierno | Winter day | Nitz-nas |
| Noche | Night | Ata-jai |
| Noche de Verano | Summer night | Nitz-atajai* |
| Noche de Invierno | Winter night | Yac-atajai |
| El amanecer | Sunrise, daybreak | Up-cus-ta-a |
| Medio día | Midday | Apeg-guene-nas |
| La tarde | Afternoon | Yac-tzut |
| El anochecer | Sunset, nightfall | Up-a-apto |
| Ayer | Yesterday | A-meo-i, Ha-mi |
| Mañana | Tomorrow | Amitla |
| Hoy | Today | Tups-hitl |
| Ahora | Now | Tla |

* In comparison with summer day and winter day it appears that this term and the following should be reversed. There may have been an error in copying.

| En el instante | At the moment | Yu-si-nic |
|---|---|---|
| Yo | I | Sia |
| Tu | You | Sua |
| Aquel | It | Tlau-tla |
| Nosotros | We | U-yahtl |
| Uno | One | Sa-huac |
| Dos | Two | A-tla |
| Tres | Three | Catza |
| Quatro | Four | Mu |
| Cinco | Five | Su-cha |
| Seis | Six | Nu-pu |
| Siete | Seven | Atli-pu |
| Ocho | Eight | Atla-cuatl |
| Nueve | Nine | Sa-hua-cual |
| Diez | Ten | Ha-yo |
| Uno solo | Only one | Tza-huitl |
| Muchos | Many | A-yi-mil |
| Cosa mia | Mine | Si-yatz |
| Cosa tuya | Yours | Suat-tzis |
| Cosa de aquel | His | Tlaut-tzis |
| Rico | Rich | Cu-as, co-as |
| Pobre | Poor | U-ua-pee, hua-hua-pee |
| | | |
| Cosa nueva | New thing | Chu-selg-xi |
| Cosa alta | High thing | Saya-cha |
| baja | Low | A-na-chas |
| poca | Small (amount) | Huis-tzu |
| llena | Full | Ca-ma |
| grande | Big | Yg-e-pu |
| chica | Little | Atl-ma-chis |
| redonda | Round | Up-qui-mitl |
| quadrada | Square | Yac-ca-mitl |
| gruesa | Thick | Huic-xa |
| delgada | Thin | Tzi-ti-yu |
| caliente | Hot | Tlug-mas |
| fria | Cold | Magtl-as |
| encarnado | Red, flesh-colored | Hi-juc |
| azul | Blue | Tup-cuc |
| verde | Green | Tlitz-mitz |
| amarilla | Yellow | Tlitz-tzuc |

| | | |
|---|---|---|
| negra | Black | Tzu-mitz |
| blanca | White | Atli-tzutl |
| Qué? | What? | A-cac |
| Quien[?] | Who? | Atzit-tza |
| En donde | Where, in which | U-yi |
| Como | Like or as | Co-co-coa |
| Quanto [?] | How much? | U-ná |
| Por qué[?] | Why? | Acanaca-coe |
| Arriba | Above | Iltz-pe |
| Abajo | Below | Us-te-el |
| En medio | In the middle | Ape-hue-ne |
| Lejos | Far | Sa-ya |
| Cerca | Near | A-nas |
| Alrededor | Around | Tut-xitl |
| A la buelta | Around the corner, on the other side | Cutz-pa |
| Si | Yes | E-o |
| No | No | Huic |

## Verbs in Alphabetical Order

| | | |
|---|---|---|
| Albofetear | To slap | Tloj-me-jujel |
| Abrazar | To embrace | Ap-qui-xitl |
| Acostarse | To go to bed | Tac-petl |
| Amar | To love | O-ca-yo |
| Andar | To walk | Yac-tzuc |
| Aprender | To learn | Amiti-amita |
| Arrojar | To hurl, throw | Huag-xitl |
| Axotar | To whip, lash | Chi-caca |
| Besar | To kiss | Temest-tzitl, Tzi-mec-t |
| Bostecear | To yawn | Ax-ec-tzitl |
| Beber | To drink | Nac-tzitl |
| Callar | To be quiet | Tza-mac |
| Cagar | To defecate | Ap-cu-itz |
| Cantar | To sing | Nu-mic |
| Cargar | To load, burden | Ap-cu-itz |
| Chanzear | To jest, poke fun | Ami-chapa |
| Comer | To eat | Au-co |
| Cambiar o comprar | To exchange or buy | Ma-cu-co |

| | | |
|---|---|---|
| Cortar el cabello | To cut the hair | Chique-me-yntl |
| Cubrirse | To cover oneself | O-cu-chas |
| Dar | To give | Pachitle |
| Derramar | To pour out, spill | Tzitz-chitl |
| Decir | To say | Si-sani |
| Decir de memoria | To say from memory | Cha-nec-titz |
| Despertar | To wake up | Asg-xitl |
| Dormir | To sleep | Hue-itche |
| Eru[p]tar | To belch | Ninitz-tzca |
| Estar | To be | Hui-na-pé |
| Estar en pie | To be standing up | Tle-quilg |
| Estar atado | To be tied up | Ma-matl-ape |
| Estar suelto | To be free, untied | Tli-ca-patl |
| Escupir | To spit | Taja-tzitl |
| Estornudar | To sneeze | Toupeg-chitl |
| Esperezarse | To stretch oneself | Tag-ya-tle |
| Entrar | To enter | Yni-itl |
| Fornicar | To fornicate | Guat-guata, Hua-huata |
| Golpear en los ojos | To hit in the eyes | Tli-qui-tzu-jutl |
| Gustar | To like | Chamai-pal |
| Gritar | To shout | A-ja-ni-yu |
| Hablar uno solo | To speak—one person | Tla-nac |
| Hablar muchos | To speak—many | Nig-tlac |
| Hacer gestos | To gesture | Chis-tzitl |
| Herirse ligeramente | To wound oneself lightly | Chic-chi-ni-etl |
| Herirse gravemente | To wound oneself gravely | Chi-algtas, Chi-althas |
| Hurtar | To steal, pilfer | Cap-xitl |
| Llamar por señas | To call by signals | Tlut-tlutl-nac |
| Lastimar el Humo | To hurt one's pride | Coit-tza |
| Lavarse | To wash oneself | Tzau-tze-nic |
| Levantar | To raise | Tzo-cuitl |
| Levantarse | To rise, get up | Tle-qui-sit |
| Llevar por la mano | To carry by hand | A-chi-nic |
| Llorar | To cry | Aei-jatl |
| Llover | To rain | Mic-tzitl |
| Matar | To kill | Cagit-tzitle |
| Matarse a si mismo | To kill oneself | Tzoc-tzitle |

| | | |
|---|---|---|
| Mear el Hombre | To urinate—man | Oc-tzitle |
| Mear la Muger | To urinate—woman | Omec-tzitl |
| Mecer | To stir, mix | Puag-tla-to |
| Oler | To smell | Mitz-mitza |
| Oir | To hear | Na-a |
| Parir | To give birth | Hei-ne-metl |
| Pasearse | To take a walk | Tutz-jutza |
| Peerse | To break wind | Huag-tzitl |
| Peinarse | To comb one's hair | Tzach-qui-nitl |
| Prestar | To loan | Acol-tli |
| Quebrar | To break | Coat-chitl |
| Quemarse | To burn oneself | Mug-chitl |
| Quemarse el cabello | To burn the hair | Atz-quimi-yutl |
| Querer | To want | A-a-coc |
| Rasgar | To tear, claw | Tzetz-qui-sitl |
| Rascarse | To scratch oneself | Niqui-ni-coa |
| Recibir | To receive | Ca-a-tli |
| Reirse | To laugh | Tlig-jo-a |
| Retozar | To frolic, play | Mi-ap |
| Robar | To steal, rob | Tzu-cuitl |
| Roncar | To snore | Op-ta |
| Sacar la lengua | To stick out the tongue | Chup-azp-tzitl |
| Salir | To leave, go out | Y-ni-as |
| Sentarse | To sit down | Tec-pitl |
| Soplar | To blow | Pug-xitl |
| Sorber | To sip | Chic-tzitl |
| Soñar | To dream | Pu-es-nac |
| Suspirar | To sigh | E-eg-tzitl, Hitl-tzitl |
| Subir | To climb, lift up | Sa-ac |
| Tener | To have | U-nac |
| Tener hambre | To be hungry | A-hue-quetl |
| Tener sed | To be thirsty | Na-ca-mejas |
| Tener sueño | To be sleepy | Po-ag-tlato |
| Tirar de la ropa | To pull by the clothing | Cu-tzit |
| Tirar del brazo | To pull by the arm | Tzu-tzu-as |
| Tocar o palpar | To touch | Tlug-tlulg-tla |
| Tocer [toser] | To cough | Huatzag-chitl |
| Trabajar | To work | Ma-muc |

| Tomar | To take, drink | Ma-atl |
|---|---|---|
| Veer [ver] | To see | Na-na-nichi |
| Verse en los ojos de otro | To see oneself in the eyes of another | Nechi-zu |
| Bomitar [Vomitar] | To vomit | Alg-alg-tla |

## Names of the months

| Enero | January | U-ya-ca-milks |
|---|---|---|
| Febrero | February | Aya-ca-milks |
| Marzo | March | Qu-cu-migl |
| Abril | April | Ca-ju-milks |
| Mayo | May | Ca-huetz-mitl |
| Junio | June | Atzetz-tzimtl |
| Julio | July | Sta-tzimelt |
| Agosto | August | Ynic-coatz-tzimitl |
| Septiembre | September | Eitz-tzutz |
| Octubre | October | Ma-mec-tzu |
| Noviembre | November | Caz-la-tic |
| Diciembre | December | A-ju-mitl |

# APPENÒIX B

*Catalogue of the animals and plants which the authorities of my expedition, Don José Moziño and Don José Maldonado, have examined and classified according to the system of Linnaeus*

[EDITOR'S NOTE: The following common names and modern scientific classifications have been supplied to suggest the fauna and flora studied by Moziño and Maldonado during their association with the Bodega y Quadra expedition in Mexico, the Pacific Northwest, and California. The Latin names recorded in 1792 illustrate a pioneer attempt to make identifications on the basis of available European descriptions within the Linnaean system. Doubtless many new species were erroneously considered identical to similar European ones or, in the absence of information, were inaccurately identified. Also, few of Moziño's new names became permanent. Other changes have resulted simply from the historical evolution of scientific classification.]

## ANIMALS

| | |
|---|---|
| *Vespertilio murinus* | bat |
| *Phoca ursina* | probably *P. fasciata*, ribbon seal |
| *vitulina* | harbor seal or common seal |
| *? lutra* | *Lutra canadensis*, river otter |

| | |
|---|---|
| *Canis mexicanus* | *Canis* includes coyote (brush wolf) and gray or timber wolf |
| *Felis lynx* | now *Lynx canadensis*, lynx |
| *Mustela lutris* | *Mustela* includes short and long-tailed weasel and mink |
| *martes* | probably *Martes americana*, martin; possibly *Martes pennanti*, the fisher |
| *herminea* | |
| *Ursus arctos* | *Ursus* includes black, big brown, and grizzly bear |
| *lotor* | |
| *luscus* | |
| *Mus terratris* | *M. musculus*, house mouse |
| *rattus* | *Rattus* now genus for black and brown rats |
| *Sciurus flabus* | *S. griseus*, western gray squirrel |
| *Cervus elaphus* | *C. canadensis*, elk or wapiti |
| *Balaena misticetus* | *B. mysticetus*, bowhead whale (Greenland or Arctic right whale) |
| *Physeter catudon* | *P. catodon*, sperm whale or cachalot |
| *Delphinus phowena* | dolphin |

### BIRDS

| | |
|---|---|
| *Falco leucocephalus* | *Haliaeetus leucocephalus*, bald eagle |
| *gyrfalco* | *F. peregrinus*, peregrine falcon |
| *sparverius* | sparrow hawk |
| *Corbus corax* | *Corvus corax*, common raven |
| *glandarius* | *C. caurinus*, Northwest crow |
| *afer* | |
| *Alcedo alcyon* | now *Megaceryle alcyon*, belted kingfisher |
| *Trochilus polytmus* | probably *Selasphorus rufus*, rufous hummingbird, or *Stellula calliope*, calliope hummingbird |
| *fulvis* | |
| *Anas cygnus* | now *A. cyanoptera*, cinnamon teal |
| *tadorna* | |
| *crecca* | common or European teal |
| *Mergus merganser* | common or American merganser |
| *Procellaria pelagica* | family of fulmars, shearwaters, and petrels |
| *fregata* | |

| | |
|---|---|
| *Diomedea demersa* | albatross |
| *Pelecanus carbo* | now *P. erythrorhynchos*, white pelican |
| *Phaeton tridactylus* | tropic bird |
| *Colymbus candidus* | small alcid, murrelet, or auklet |
| *Larus canus* | mew or short-billed gull |
| *Sterna bucarelia* | tern |
| *Ardea grus* | sandhill crane? |
| ciconia | *A. herodias*, great blue heron |
| cinerea | |
| cocoi | possibly a kind of bittern |
| *Tringa hyperborea* | *Phalaropus lobatus*, northern phalarope |
| *Charadrius plubialis* | *Pluvialis dominica*, golden plover |
| torquatus | *C. vociferus*, killdeer |
| *Phasianos nanaquios* | *Phasianus* sp., pheasant |
| *Tetrao californica* | *Lophortyx*, California quail |
| *Columba oenas* | pigeon |
| leucocephala | now *Patagioenas leucocephala*, white-headed pigeon |
| turtur | |
| *Alauda campestris* | *A. arvensis*, skylark |
| natzape | possibly horned lark |
| *Sturnus californicus* | *S. vulgaris*, starling (European species); possibly a kind of finch |
| *Turdus dominicus* | probably *Ixoreus noevius noevius*, varied thrush (winter robin) |
| *Loxia curbirostra* | *L. curvirostra*, red crossbill |
| *Motacilla schoenotaens* | possibly yellow or white wagtail or wheatear |
| atricapilla | |

AMPHIBIANS [REPTILE]

| | |
|---|---|
| *Coluber nutkensis* | *C. constrictor*, racer |

[FISH]

| | |
|---|---|
| *Raia batis* | *Raja* sp., skate |
| *Squalus zigaena* | *Sphyrna zygaena*, smooth hammerhead shark |
| *Balistes vetula* | probably *B. polylepis*, finescale triggerfish |

[ 113 ]

| | |
|---|---|
| *Diodon hystrix* | porcupine fish |
| *Muraena helena* | moray eel |
| *ophis* | *Ophichthus triserialis*, Pacific snake eel |
| *Xiphias gladius* | swordfish |
| *Cottus cinereus* | sculpin |
| *Pleuronectes linguatla* | lefteye flounder |
| *rhombus* | lefteye flounder |
| *dentatus* | *Paralichthys dentatus*, California halibut |
| *maximus* | halibut? |
| *maior* | |
| *Perca fluviatilis* | European freshwater perch |
| *lucioperca* | European freshwater perch |
| *punctatus* | |
| *nobilis* | |
| *formosa* | |
| *virgo* | |
| *Scomber thynnus* | possibly *Thunnus thynnus*, bluefin tuna |
| *Trigla hirund* | sea robin |
| *Cobitis imberbis* | loach? |
| *Salmo saurus* | salmon |
| *immaculatus* | salmon |
| *Esox brasiliensis* | pike? |
| *Cyprinus americanus* | probably a kind of minnow |

INSECTS

| | |
|---|---|
| *Dermestes murinus* | *D. caninus*, larder beetle |
| *Ptinus pertinax**  | spider beetle |
| *Elater niger**  | click beetle |
| *Meloe vesicatorius**  | blister beetle |
| *Staphilinus maxillosus**  | rove beetle |
| *variegatus**  | rove beetle |
| *Mantis virescens* | preying mantid |
| *Griyos unicolor* | *Gryllus*, cricket |
| *campestris* | cricket |
| *Coccus uvae ursi* | a scale insect |
| *Papilio brassicae**  | butterfly of a group called "whites" |
| *Libellula quadrimaculata**  | dragonfly |
| *aenea**  | dragonfly |
| *Vespa vulgaris**  | hornet |

\* European species.

| | |
|---|---|
| *Musca plevcia* | fly |
| *domestica* | common house fly |
| *maculata* | fly |
| *Culex pipiens* | common house mosquito |
| *Pediculus humanus* | human louse |

**[TESTACEAN]**

| | |
|---|---|
| *Cancer hexapas* | crab |
| *pelagicus* | |
| *maenas* | |
| *bernhardus*\* | hermit crab |
| *diogenes* | hermit crab |
| *tubularis* | |
| *Scolopendra morsitanus* | centipede |

**WORMS**

| | |
|---|---|
| *Hirudo heteroclus* | leech? |
| *Limax albus* | slug |
| *agrestis* | |
| *flabus* | |
| *Actinia equina* | possibly sea anemone |
| *senilis* | |
| *Holothuria priapus* | sea cucumber (echinoderm) |
| *Sepia officinalis* | cuttlefish (cephalopod |
| *sepiola* | |
| *Medusa oruciata* | medusa (coelenterate) |
| *Asterias rubens* | starfish |
| *reticulata* | |
| *ophiura* | probably brittle star |

**TESTACEAN [SHELLFISH]**

| | |
|---|---|
| *Chiton tuberculatus* | chiton |
| *Lepas anatifera* | goose barnacle |
| *diadema* | *Cornula dissema*, sessile barnacle |
| *Pholas dactylus* | piddock or angel wing |
| *punillus* | |
| *Donax striata* | bean clam |
| *Venus verrucosa* | *Pitar lupanaria*, Venus clam |

\* European species.

[ 115 ]

| | |
|---|---|
| *gallina* | |
| *eryana* | |
| *meretrix* | *Meretrix meretrix* |
| *Ostrea jacobaea* | oyster |
| *Mytilus edulis* | bay mussel |
| *Argonauta argo* | probably paper nautilus (cephalopod) |
| *Buccinum echinophorum* | whelk? |
| *Murex rana* | frog shell |
| *olearium* | triton |
| *femorale* | |
| *Trochus maculatus* | top shell |
| *perspectivus* | |
| *Haliotis tuberculata* | abalone |
| *Patella fusca* | limpet |
| *graeca* | |
| *nimbosa* | |
| *Madrepora agaricus* | coral? |
| *Aleyonium arboreum* | probably soft coral |
| *Spongia flabelliformis* | a kind of sponge |
| *Vorticella encrinus* | protozoan |
| *polypina* | |
| *ovifera* | |

## PLANTS*

| | |
|---|---|
| *Veronica biloba* | speedwell |
| *Justicia minima* | justicia |
| *Circaea alpina* | enchanter's nightshade |
| *Valeriana celtica* | valerian |
| *cornucopiae* | |
| *sibirica* | |
| *Agrostis sylvatica* | bent grass |
| *Aira aquatica* | hairgrass |
| *Bronus secalinus* | *Bromus*, chess grass or cheat grass |
| *Avena sibirica* | straw |
| *Hordeum bulgare* | *H. vulgare*, common barley |
| *Plantago maior* | *P. major*, common plantain |
| *maritima* | seaside plantain |

* Common names and modern classifications supplied by Professor Gordon A. Clopine.

| | |
|---|---|
| *alpina* | alpine plantain |
| *Gallium uliginosum* | *Galium*, bedstraw or cleavers |
| *aparine* | |
| *Cornus canadiensis* | bunchberry or Canadian dogwood |
| *Santalum album* | sandalwood |
| *Acaena elongata* | common acaena |
| *Potamopeton natans* | *Potamogeton*, pondweed |
| *Lithospermun officinale* | gromwell or puccoon |
| *Borrago officinalis* | |
| *Anagallis arvensis* | common pimpernel |
| *Dodecatheon meadia* | shooting star |
| *Phlox pinnatifida* | phlox |
| *Azalea nutkensis* | azalea |
| *Capsicum annum* | pepper |
| *Solanum aethiopicum* | *Solanum* sp., nightshade |
| *tuberosum* | potato |
| *poniferum* | |
| *havanense* | |
| *nigrum* | black nightshade, morel |
| *Campanula linearis* | bellflower? (*C. rotundifolia*, harebell) |
| *Lonicera symphoricarpus* | honeysuckle |
| *nutkensis* | |
| *Ceanothus borealis* | California lilac |
| *Claytonia sibirica* | springbeauty (perhaps *Montia sibirica*) |
| *linearis* | springbeauty (perhaps *Montia linearis*) |
| *Ribes vua orispa* | currant or gooseberry |
| *racemosa* | |
| *Glaux maritima* | sea milkwort |
| *Heuchera americana* | alumroot |
| *Salsola sativa* | summer cypress? (possibly *Bassia* or *Kochia*) |
| *Chenopodium hybridium* | now *C. gigantospermum*, goosefoot or pigweed |
| *bonus henricus* | goosefoot |
| *Beta vulgaris* | garden beet |
| *Hydrocotyle vulgaris* | marsh pennywort |
| *Daucus carota* | wild carrot or Queen Anne's lace |
| *muricatus* | Moorish carrot |
| *Lasserpitium latifolium* | *Laserpitium* |
| *Angelica archangelica* | angelica |

| | |
|---|---|
| *silvestris* | |
| *Cicuta virosa* | water hemlock |
| *Pastinaca sativa* | parsnip |
| *Apium graveolens* | celery |
| *Sambucus nigra* | elderberry |
| *racemosa* | now *S. melanocarpa*, elderberry |
| *Allium nutans* | wild onion |
| *graveolens* | |
| *sibiricum* | |
| *cepa* | chive |
| *Convallaria bifolia* | now *Smilacina*, false Solomon's seal |
| *Asphodelus luteus* | perhaps related to *Narthecium*, adder's tongue or fawnlily |
| *Erythonium denscanis* | dogtooth lily |
| *Vualaria amplexicaulis* | |
| *Lilium kamschatkense* | lily |
| *Rumex orispa* | dock or sorrel |
| *maritima* | *R. fueginus*, golden dock |
| *Trientalis europaea* | *T. latifolia*, star flower |
| *Epilobium tetragonum* | genus known as willow herb |
| *angustifolium* | fireweed |
| *longifolium* | |
| *montanum* | |
| *palustre* | |
| *Vaccinium arctostaphilus* | genus includes huckleberry, bilberry, and blueberry |
| *vitis idaea* | rock cranberry |
| *oxicoccus* | |
| *Poligonum persicaria* | *Polygonum*, lady's thumb |
| *Pirola umbellata* | *Pyrola* |
| *uniflora* | wood nymph |
| *Ledum septrentrionale* | ledum (closely related to Labrador tea) |
| *Andromeda racemosa* | marsh andromeda |
| *Kalmia glauca* | American laurel |
| *Arbutus unedo* | strawberry tree or madrone |
| *vita ursi* | |
| *alpina* | |
| *Mentziena ferruginea* | possibly *Mentzelia*, blazing star |
| *Saxifraga cotyledon* | *Saxifragia*, saxifrage |
| *Tiarella trifoliata* | sugar scoop |

| | |
|---|---|
| *Mitela diphylla* | mitterwort or bishop's cap |
| *Arenaria media* | now *Spergularia*, sand spurrey |
| *verna* | |
| *triflora* | three-nerved sandwort |
| *Stellaria dichothoma* | chickweed or starwort |
| *graminea* | |
| *Cotyledon hispanica* | perhaps *Dudleya*, live forever |
| *Sedum hybridum* | stonecrop or orpin |
| *verticillatuns* | |
| *nutkense* | |
| *Oxalis violacea* | wood sorrel |
| *flabelliformis* | |
| *linearis* | |
| *Portulaca oloracea* | purslane |
| *Prunus nutkensis* | stonefruits |
| *Sorbus simplicifolius* | mountain ash |
| *Pirus baccata* | possibly *P. rivularis*, Oregon crabapple |
| *Spiraea opulifolia* | spiraea; possibly rock spiraea, goat-beard, desert sweet, meadowsweet ocean spray |
| *chamedrifolia* | |
| *crenata* | |
| *salicifolia* | |
| *Rosa gallica* | *R. nutkana*, Nootka rose |
| *Rubus idaecus* | genus includes blackberry, raspberry, salmonberry, thimbleberry |
| *muluccanus* | |
| *hispidus* | |
| *Fragaria vesca* | now *F. chiloensis*, beach strawberry |
| *Potentila nivea* | *Potentilla*, cinquefoil or five-finger |
| *anserina* | |
| *Geum barbarum* | avens |
| *Papaber somniferum* | *Papaver*, opium poppy |
| *Nymphaea lutea* | probably *Nuphar polysepalum*, cowlily or pond lily |
| *Ranunculus pensilvanus* | buttercup or crowfoot |
| *Adonis puerulus* | possibly larkspur, Indian cress, or nasturtium |
| *Aguilia viscosa* | |
| *Menta sativa* | *Mentha*, mint |

| | |
|---|---|
| *pulegium* | pennyroyal |
| *Stachis sylvatica* | *Stachys*, hedge nettle |
| *Prunella vulgaris* | selfheal (sometimes written *Brunella*) |
| *Mellisa nepeta* | *Melissa* sp., balm |
| *Orobanche americana* | broomrape |
| *Scrophularia marilandica* | figwort |
| *Anthirrynum junceum* | *Antirrhinum*, snapdragon |
| *Mimulos luteus* barbatus | now *Mimulus nasutus*, monkeyflower |
| *Linaea americana* | *Linnaea*, twinflower |
| *Castilleja pulcherrima* | paintbrush |
| *Subularia aquatica* | awlwort |
| *Iberis gibraltarica* | candytuft |
| *Alissum minimum* | probably *Alyssum lobularia*, sweet alyssum |
| *Clipeola mexicana* | *Clypeola* |
| *Raphanus satibus* | *R. sativus*, wild radish |
| *Erysimum vulgare* | wallflower |
| *Brassica violacea* | mustard |
| alpina | mustard |
| napus | rape |
| oleracea | cabbage |
| *Sinapus arvensis* | now *Brassica arvensis*, var. *pinnatifida*, kaber |
| *Sisymbrium nasturtium* | now *Nasturtium officinale*, water cress |
| *Geranium sibiricum* | cranesbill |
| *Malva rotundifolia* | mallow, cheeses |
| *Fumaria cucullata* sempervirens | fulmitory |
| *Phaseolus vulgaris* | bean |
| *Pisum maritimum* | now *Lathyrus japonicus*, pea |
| *Lathyrus aphaca* angulatus | pea |
| *Vicia faba* | vetch, horsebean |
| *Trifolium repens* | clover |
| *Cicer arietinum* | chick-pea |
| *Sonchus aruensis* sibiricus alpinus | sow thistle |
| *Lactuca sativa* | garden lettuce |

| | |
|---|---|
| *serriola* | prickly lettuce |
| *Cynara scolimus* | *C. scolymus*, artichoke |
| *Cardus lanceolatus* | now *Cirsium*, thistle |
| *latuiginosus* | |
| *Cacalia sarracenica* | probably *Cacaliopsis* |
| *albifrons* | |
| *Gnaphalium margaricacium* | now *Anaphalis margaritacea*, pearly ever-lasting |
| *pedunculare* | |
| *Matricaria maritima* | now *Chrysanthemum*, sunflower family |
| *parthenium* | |
| *chamonnilla* | |
| *Solidago virga aurea* | goldenrod |
| *mexicana* | |
| *Aster laebis* | aster |
| *sibiricus* | |
| *Helenium pinnatifidum* | sneezeweed |
| *Achilea millefolium* | *Achillea*, common yarrow |
| *Viola odarata* | English violet |
| *Satyrium capense* | |
| *Serapias rubia* | now *Eburophyton*, phanton orchid |
| *Sisyrinchium bermuda* | Bermuda grass |
| *Arum obatum* | arum |
| *virginianum* | |
| *Urtica divica* | nettle |
| *Betula alnus* | birch or alder |
| *Ambrosia artemisiifolia* | low ragweed |
| *Amaranthus cruentus* | amaranth |
| *Sagitaria sagittifolia* | arrowhead |
| *Poterium sanguisorba* | now *Sanguisorba minor*, burnet |
| *Pinus sylvestres* | pine (many species possibilities) |
| *cathadienus* | |
| *abies* | |
| *pinea* | |
| *orientalis* | |
| *Cupressus thyvides* | cypress |
| *Thuja dolabrata* | possibly *T. plicata* or *T. gigantea*, red cedar |
| *Salix incubacea* | willow |
| *Myrica gale* | waxmyrtle |

| | |
|---|---|
| *Acer pseudoplatanus* | maple |
| *Equisetum sylvaticum* | scouring rush or horsetail |
| *arvense* | common horsetail |
| *Osmunda lunaria* | probably Blechnum, deer fern |
| *Acrostichum septentrionale* | *Achrosticum*, common ceterach, milt-waste |
| *Blechnum virginium* | deer fern |
| *orientale* | |
| *Asplenius caterach* | spleenwort |
| *Polypodium vulgare* | polypody, licorice fern |
| *parisiticum* | |
| *cristatum* | |
| *felix mas* | |
| *Adianthum capillus venerus* | *Adiantum*, Venus-hair fern |
| *Polytrichum ammune* | probably holly or sword fern |
| *Minium pelluadium* | true moss |
| *Bryum extinctenum* | moss, liverwort, or hornwort |
| *rurale* | |
| *muralle* | |
| *alpinum* | |
| *Jungermania fulgen.* | leafy liverwort |
| *Lichen nivalis* | now *Cetraria*, lichen |
| *caperatus* | now *Parmelia caperata*, lichen |
| *perlatus* | now *Parmelia perlata*, lichen |
| *cocciferus* | now *Cladonia coccifera*, lichen |
| *lanatus* | now *Parmelia lanata* or *Ephebe lanata*, lichen |
| *pubescens* | now *Parmelia lanata* or *Ephebe lanata*, lichen |
| *tartareus* | now *Ochrolechia tartarea*, lichen |
| *Tremella difformis* | jelly fungi |
| *Fucus natans* | rockweed? |
| *ovaricus* | |
| *elongarus* | |
| *buccinalis* | |
| *Ulva latissima* | sea lettuce (green alga) |
| *Conferva ribularis* | *C. tribonema*, yellow green alga, threaded alga |
| *bullosa* | |
| *littoralis* | |

| | |
|---|---|
| *gelatinosa* | |
| *Agaricus integer* | (fungi) mushroom |
| *muscarius* | |
| *dentatus* | |
| *campestris* | common edible mushroom |
| *fimetarius* | |
| *umbelliferus* | |
| *clabus* | |
| *Boletus versicolor* | true polypore |
| *fomentarius* | shelf fungus |
| *Hydnum parasiticum* | coral fungus |
| *Phallius impudicus* | *Phallus,* stinkhorn |
| *Helvella mitra* | saddle fungus |
| *Peziza auricula* | cup fungus |
| *Lycoperdon variolosum* | puffball |
| *truncatum* | earth star |
| *Mucor lichenoides* | black mold |

# bibliogRaphy

## UNPUBLISHED MANUSCRIPT SOURCES

[Alcalá Galiano, Dionísio, and Cayetano Valdés.] "Relación del viaje hecho por las Goletas Sutil y Mexicana en el año de 1792 para reconocer el estrecho de Fuca." Museo Naval, Madrid, MS 468.

"Antiguedades de los oficiales de guerra de la Armada." Museo Naval, Madrid, MS 1161.

"Bocabulario de varias vozes que pronuncian los Indios en la Costa Septentrional de California, segun la obra de Cook." Museo Naval, Madrid, MS 331.

Bodega y Quadra, Juan Francisco de la. Letter of Bodega y Quadra to Francisco Eliza, "Instrucciones secretas," February 4, 1791. Archivo General de la Nación, Mexico, D.F., Historia 69.

———. "Navegación hecha por don Juan Francisco de la Bodega y Quadra, Teniente de Fragata de la Real Armada y Comandante de la Goleta *Sonora*, a los descubrimientos de los Mares y Costa Septentrional de California [1775]." Museo Naval, Madrid, MS 622.

———. "Viaje a la Costa N. O. de la America Septentrional por Don Juan Francisco de la Bodega y Quadra, del Orden de Santiago, Capitan de Navío de la Real Armada, y Comandante del Departamento de San Blas en las Fragatas de su mando *Sta. Gertrudis, Aranzazu, Princesa* y Goleta *Activo* en el año de 1792." Archivo del Ministerio de Asuntos Exteriores, Madrid, MS 145, and Revilla Gigedo Papers, Vol. XXIX, Private Collection of Irving W. Robbins, Atherton, Calif.

Caamaño, Jacinto. "Extracto del Diario de las navegaciones, exploraciones y descubrimientos hechos en la America Septentrional por D. Jacinto Caamaño." Archivo del Ministerio de Asuntos Exteriores, Madrid, MS 10.

# Bibliography

"Catálogo de los Animales y Plantas que han reconocido y determinado segun el sistema de Linneo los Facultativos de mi Expedición Don José Moziño y Don José Maldonado." Archivo del Ministerio de Asuntos Exteriores, Madrid, MS 145; Revilla Gigedo Papers, Vol. XXIX, Private Collection of Irving W. Robbins, Atherton, Calif.

"Copia de la orden instructiva comunicada al Alferez graduado de Navío Estevan José Martínez para su gobierno y observancia en la Ocupación del Puerto de San Lorenzo o Nutka." Archivo Histórico Nacional, Madrid, Estado 4289.

"Extracto de la navegación que ha hecho el piloto Don Juan Pantoja y Arriaga en el paquebot de S. M. el San Carlos . . . desde San Blas el 4 de Febrero de 1791." Museo Naval, Madrid, MS 271.

Gregorio, Bishop José. Letter of Bishop José Gregorio to Doña María Rita Rivera, Oaxaca, August 14, 1790. Archivo General de la Nación, Mexico, D.F., Historia 465.

Malaspina, Alejandro, and José Bustamante y Guerra. "Plan de un Viaje Científico y Político al Rededor del Mundo Remitido a el Exmo. Sr. Bailio Fray Antonio Valdes de Madrid en Sept. 10 de 1788." Museo Naval, Madrid, MS 316.

Martínez, Esteban José. "Diario de la Navegación que Yo el Alferez de Navio de la Real Armada Dn. Estevan Josef Martínez voy a executar al Puerto de San Lorenzo de Nuca, mandando la Fragata Princesa, y Paquebot San Carlos de Orden de el Exmo. Sor. Dn. Manuel Antonio Florez, Virrey, Governador y Capitan general de N. España en el presente año de 1789." Museo Naval, Madrid, MS 732. See also Barreiro-Meiro, ed., [Diario de] Esteban José Martínez (1742–1798), under Published Sources and References.

———. "Viaje executado por el Piloto Estevan José Martínez en la Fragata Santiago alias la Nueva Galicia propria de S. M. y por orden del Exmo. Sor. Baylio Fr. Dn. Antonio Maria Bucareli . . . a la altura de 55 grados norte . . . en 24 dias del mes de Henero de 1774." Archivo General de Indias, Sevilla, Guadalajara, 516.

Moziño, José Mariano. "Breve Diccionario de los terminos que se pudieran aprender del idioma de los naturales de Nutka." Archivo del Ministerio de Asuntos Exteriores, Madrid, MS 145.

———. "Descripción de la isla de Mazarredo, junto a la Quadra o Vancouver y noticias de aquellos países." Museo Naval, Madrid, MSS 143 and 468.

———. Letter of Moziño to Pedro Cevallos, Madrid, October 24, 1808.

# Bibliography

Archivo del Museo Nacional de Ciencias Naturales, Madrid, Flora Espanola—Año 1808.

———. "Noticias de Nutca por Don Jose Moziño, Botánico de la expedición de N[ueva] E[spaña] y la de limites al norte de Californias año de 1793." Revilla Gigedo Papers, Volume XXX, Private Collection of Irving W. Robbins, Atherton, Calif.

———. "Relación de la Isla de Mazarredo." Frederick W. Beinecke Collection, Yale University Library, New Haven, Conn.

"Orden del Rey Carlos IV," 1792, 4ª Division, Legajo No. 15. Archivo del Real Jardin Botánico, Madrid.

Pérez, Juan. "Continuación del Diario que formó el alferez graduado de Fragata Don Juan Perez, Primer Piloto del Departamento de San Blas, con la titulada 'Santiago' alias 'la Nueva Galicia' de su mando. . . . a explorar la costa Septentrional y su regreso. . . . ," August 26, 1774. Archivo General de Indias, Sevilla, Estado 38.

———. "Diario de la Navegación hecha por el Alferez Graduado D. Juan Perez de ord. del Sr. Bucareli a la altura de los grados donde esta situada la entrada y Bahia de su nombre en la fragata Santiago, alias la Nª Galicia, San Blas, 3 de Noviembre de 1774." Museo Naval, Madrid, MSS 331, 575 bis, Archivo General de la Nación, Mexico, D.F., Historia 62.

"Planos geográficos y dibujos para ilustrar el Diario de D. Juan Francisco de la Bodega y Quadra." Archivo del Ministerio de Asuntos Exteriores, Madrid, MS 146; Revilla Gigedo Papers, Vol. XXIX, Private Collection of Irving W. Robbins, Atherton, Calif.

Quimper, Manuel. "Pequeño Bocabulario dada por D. Manuel Quimper de los havitantes comprendidos entre los 48 y 50 grados de latitud en su viaje al reconocimiento del Estrecho de Fuca el ano 1790." Museo Naval, Madrid, MS 331.

"Relación del Viaje hecho por las Goletas Sutil y Mexicana en el año de 1792." See Alcalá Galiano and Valdés.

Revilla Gigedo, Conde de. Letter of Revilla Gigedo to Duque de Alcudia, Mexico, April 12, 1793. Revilla Gigedo Papers, Vol. XIII, Private Collection of Irving W. Robbins, Atherton, Calif.

———. Letter of Revilla Gigedo to Florida Blanca, Mexico, November 12, 1791. Archivo General de Indias, Sevilla, Estado 20.

———. Letter of Revilla Gigedo to Juan Francisco de la Bodega y Quadra, Mexico, October 29, 1791, Archivo Histórico Nacional, Madrid, Estado 4287.

# Bibliography

Santelices Pablo, Juan Eugenio. Letter of Santelices Pablo to Josef de Espinoza, Mexico, March 16, 1791. Additional MSS. No. 17631, Archives of the British Museum, London.

"Segunda Exploración de la Costa Septentrional de la California en 1775 con la Fragata Santiago y Goleta Sonora, mandado por el Teniente de Navio D. Bruno de Heceta y de Fragata D. Juan de la [Bodega y] Quadra desde el Puerto de San Blas hasta los 58 grados de latitud." Museo Naval, Madrid, MS 331.

Sessé, Martín. Letter of Martín Sessé to Viceroy Revilla Gigedo, Mexico, May 9, 1793. Archivo General de la Nación, Mexico, D.F., Historia 527.

"Tercera exploración de la Costa Septentrional de Californias con las dos Fragatas Princesa y Faborita, mandadas por el Teniente de Navio D. Ignacio Arteaga, y por el de la misma clase D. Juan de la [Bodega y] Quadra en el año de 79 desde el Puerto de San Blas hasta los 61 grados de Latitud." Museo Naval, Madrid, MS 331.

"Testimonio del Expediente sobre haberse resuelto que el Botánico Don Jaime Senseve quede en Mexico y que en su lugar salga con la Expedición el Medico Dn. Jose Mosiño, nombrado para la disección de los animales al Cirujano Maldonado." Archivo del Museo de Ciencias Naturales, Madrid, Flora Española—Año 1790.

## PUBLISHED SOURCES AND REFERENCES

Alcázar Molina, Cayetano. *Historia de América y de los Pueblos Americanos: Los Virreinatos en el Siglo XVIII.* Edited by Antonio Ballesteros y Beretta. Barcelona: Editores Salvat, 1945.

Anderson, Bern. *The Life and Voyages of Captain George Vancouver.* Seattle: University of Washington Press, 1960.

Andía y Varela, José de. *Relación del viaje hecho a la isla de Amat, por otro nombre Otahiti, y descubrimientos de otras adyacentes en los años 1774 y 1775.* Edited by Joaquin de Sarriera. Barcelona: J. Porter, 1947.

Arias Divito, Juan Carlos. *Las Expediciones Científicas Españolas durante el siglo XVIII: Expedición Botánica de Nueva España.* Madrid: Ediciones Cultura Hispánica, 1968.

Bancroft, Hubert H. *History of the Northwest Coast.* San Francisco: A. L. Bancroft and Co., 1884.

Barreiro-Meiro, Roberto (ed.). *[Diario de] Esteban José Martínez (1742–1798).* Colección de Diarios y Relaciones para la Historia de los Viajes y Descubrimientos, VI. Madrid: Instituto Histórico de Marina, 1964. See also Martínez, "Diario de la navegación . . . año de 1789," under Unpublished Manuscript Sources.

Brown, Robert (ed). *The Adventures and Sufferings of John Jewitt; only survivor of the crew of the ship, Boston, during a captivity of nearly three years among the Indians of Nootka Sound in Vancouver Island.* London: C. Wilson, 1896.

Candolle, Alphonse Louis de (ed.). *Calques des dessins de la Flore du Mexique de Mociño et Sessé qui ont servi de types d'especes dans le Systema ou le Prodomus.* Geneva, 1874.

——— (ed). *Memoires et souvenirs de Augustin-Pyramus de Candolle.* Geneva, 1862.

Carreño, Alberto B. (ed.). *Noticias de Nutka.* Mexico, D.F.: Sociedad Mexicana de Geografía y Estadística, 1913.

Colmeiro, Miguel. *La Botánica y los Botánicos de la Península Hispano-Lusitana.* Madrid: Imprenta y Estereotípia de M. Rivadeneyra, 1858.

Cook, James, and James King. *A Voyage to the Pacific Ocean Undertaken by the Command of His Majesty, for Making Discoveries in the Northern Hemisphere in the Years 1776, 1777, 1778, 1779, and 1780.* 3 vols. and Atlas. London: G. Nicol and T. Cadell, 1784.

Corney, Bolton Glanville. *The Quest and Occupation of Tahiti by Emissaries of Spain, 1772–1776.* London: Printed for the Hakluyt Society, 1913.

Cutter, Donald C. (ed). *The California Coast: A Bilingual Edition of Documents from the Sutro Collection.* Norman: University of Oklahoma Press, 1969.

———. "California, Training Ground for Spanish Naval Heroes," *California Historical Society Quarterly,* XL (June, 1961), 109–22.

———. *Malaspina in California.* San Francisco: John Howell—Books, 1960.

———. "Spanish Scientific Exploration along the Pacific Coast," in *The American West—An Appraisal,* edited by Robert G. Ferris. Santa Fe: Museum of New Mexico Press, 1963.

Densmore, Frances. *Nootka and Quileute Music.* Smithsonian Institution Bureau of American Ethnology Bulletin 124. Washington, D.C.: U.S. Government Printing Office, 1939.

Dixon, George. *A Voyage Round the World but more particularly to the North-West Coast of American performed in 1785, 1786, 1787, and 1788 in the King George and the Queen Charlotte: Captains Portlock and Dixon.* London: George Goulding Publisher, 1789.

Drucker, Philip. *Cultures of the North Pacific Coast.* San Francisco: Chandler Publishing Company, 1965.

———. *Indians of the Northwest Coast.* Garden City, N.Y.: Natural History Press, 1963.

———. *The Northern and Central Nootkan Tribes.* Smithsonian Institution Bureau of American Ethnology Bulletin 144. Washington, D.C.: U.S. Government Printing Office, 1951.

Eardley, A. J. *Structural Geology of North America.* New York: Harper Brothers, 1951.

Espinosa y Tello, José (ed.). *Relación del viaje hecho por las goletas Sutil y Mexicana en el año 1792.* Madrid: Imprenta Real, 1802. Reprinted in Colección Chimalistac. Madrid: José Porrúa Turanzas, 1958. See also Alcalá Galiano and Valdés, "Relacion del viaje . . . en el año 1792," under Unpublished Manuscript Sources.

*Gazeta de México,* Vol. III (December 22, 1789).

Guest, Florian. "The Establishment of the Villa de Branciforte," *California Historical Society Quarterly,* XLI (March, 1962), 29–50.

Gunther, Erna. *Art in the Life of the Northwest Indians.* Seattle: Superior Publishing Company, 1966.

Gutiérrez Camarena, Marcial. *San Blas y las Californias.* Mexico, D.F.: Editorial Jus., 1956.

Holm, Bill. *Northwest Coast Indian Art: An Analysis of Form.* Seattle: University of Washington Press, 1965.

Howay, Frederic W. (ed.). *The Dixon-Meares Controversy.* Toronto: Ryerson Press, 1929.

———. "The Dog's Hair Blankets of the Coast Salish," *Washington Historical Quarterly,* IX (April, 1918), 83–92.

———. "The Early Literature of the Northwest Coast," *Transactions of the Royal Society of Canada,* Vol. XVIII (May, 1924).

——— (ed.). *The Journal of Captain James Colnett Aboard the Argonaut from April 26, 1789, to November 3, 1791.* Toronto, Ont.: The Champlain Society, 1940.

———. "The Voyage of the *Hope:* 1790–1792," *Washington Historical Quarterly,* XI (January, 1920), 3–29.

———. "Voyages of Kendrick and Gray in 1787–90," *Oregon Historical Quarterly,* XXX (June, 1929), 89–94.

———. (ed.). *Voyages of the "Columbia" to the Northwest Coast, 1787–1790 and 1790–1793.* Massachusetts Historical Society Collections, LXXIX. Cambridge, Mass.: Harvard University Press, 1941.

Humboldt, Alexander von. *Ensayo Político sobre el Reino de la Nueva*

# Bibliography

*España*. Edited by Juan A. Ortega y Medina. Mexico, D.F.: Editorial Porrua, SA., 1966.

Inverarity, Robert Bruce. *Art of the Northwest Coast Indians*. Berkeley and Los Angeles: University of California Press, 1967.

Jewitt, John R. *A narrative of the adventures and sufferings of John R. Jewitt; only survivor of the crew of the ship, Boston, during a captivity of nearly three years among the savages of Nootka Sound: with an account of the manners, mode of living, and religious opinions of the natives*. Middletown, Conn.: Printed by Loomis and Richards, 1815.

Krause, Aurel. *The Tlingit Indians*. Translated by Erna Gunther. Seattle: University of Washington Press, 1956.

Kuhnel, Josef. *Thaddaeus Haenke, Leben und Wirken eines Forschers*. Prague: Verlag Robert Lerche Munchen Vormals Calvelsche Universitatsbuch-handlung, 1960.

La Pérouse, Jean François Galaup, Compte de. *A Voyage around the World in the Years 1785, 1787 and 1788*. 3 vols. London: J. Johnson, 1799.

Manning, William R. "The Nootka Sound Controversy," *American Historical Association Annual Report for 1904*, pp. 279–478. Washington, D.C.: U.S. Government Printing Office, 1905.

Meany, Edmond S. *Vancouver's Discovery of Puget Sound*. New York: Macmillan Co., 1907.

Meares, John. *The Memorial of John Mear[e]s to the House of Commons respecting the capture of vessels in Nootka Sound (dated April 30, 1790 and presented May 13, 1790)*. Edited by Nellie B. Pipes. Portland, Ore.: Metropolitan Press, 1933.

———. *Voyages Made in the Years 1788 and 1789 from China to the North-West Coast of America*. London: Logographic Press, 1790.

Merrill, Elmer Drew. *The Botany of Cook's Voyages*. Chronica Botanica, XIV. Waltham, Mass.: Chronica Botanica Co., 1954.

Moziño, José Mariano. "De la Polygala mexicana," *Anales de Ciencias naturales* (Madrid), Vol. VII (February, 1804).

———. "Discurso dicho en la apertura de las lecciones de Botánica en Mexico el 15 de junio de 1801," *Gaceta de Literatura de Mexico*, September, 1801, Nos. 42 and 43.

———. "Observaciones sobre la resina del Ule," *Anales de Ciencias naturales* (Madrid), Vol. VII (April, 1804).

Munford, James K. (ed.). *John Ledyard's Journal of Captain Cook's Last Voyage*. Corvallis: Oregon State University Press, 1963.

# Bibliography

Newcombe, C. F. (ed.). *Menzie's Journal of Vancouver's Voyage April to October, 1792*. Victoria, B.C.: W. H. Cullin, 1923.

Novo y Colson, Pedro de. *La Vuelta al Mundo por las Corbetas Descubierta y Atrevida al Mando del Capitán de Navío D. Alejandro Malaspina desde 1789 a 1794*. Madrid: Depósito Hidrográfico, 1885.

Rickett, Harold W. "The Royal Botanical Expedition to New Spain," *Chronica Botanica*, XI (1947), 1–87.

Santamaria, Francisco J. *Diccionario General de Americanismos*. Mexico, D.F.: Editorial Pedro Robredo, 1942.

Sapir, Edward. "A Girl's Puberty Ceremony among the Nootka Indians," *Transactions of the Royal Society of Canada*, Ser. 3, VII (1913), 67–80.

———. "Some Aspects of Nootka Language and Culture," *American Anthropologist*, XIII (1911), 15–28.

Senate Document, 32d Congress, 1st Session, *Report of Committee*, No. 335, 1852.

Servín, Manuel P. "Instructions of Viceroy Bucareli to Ensign Juan Pérez," *California Historical Society Quarterly*, XXXX (September 1961), 237–48.

Sessé y Lacasta, Martín de, and José Mariano Mociño. *Flora Mexicana*. Mexico, D. F.: Sociedad Mexicana de Historia Natural, 1885.

———. *Plantae Novae Hispaniae*. Mexico, D.F.: Sociedad Mexicana de Historia Natural, 1889.

Simpson, Lesley Byrd (ed.). *Journal of José Longinos Martínez: Notes and Observations of the Naturalist of the Botanical Expedition in Old and New California and the South Coast 1791–92*. San Francisco: John Howell—Books, 1961.

Synge, M. B. (ed.). *Captain Cook's Voyages round the World*. London: T. Nelson and Sons, 1897.

Thurman, Michael E. *The Naval Department of San Blas: New Spain's Bastion for Alta California and Nootka 1767 to 1798*. Glendale, Calif.: Arthur H. Clark Company, 1967.

Vancouver, George. *A Voyage of Discovery to the North Pacific Ocean and round the World*. 3 vols. London: C. J. and J. Robinson; J. Edwards, 1798.

Wagner, Henry R. *Cartography of the Northwest Coast of America to the Year 1800*. Vol. I. Amsterdam: N. Israel, 1968.

———. *The Last Spanish Exploration of the Northwest Coast and the Attempt to Colonize Bodega Bay*. San Francisco, 1931.

————. *Spanish Explorations in the Strait of Juan de Fuca.* Santa Ana, Tex.: Fine Arts Press, 1933.

Wagner, Henry R., and W. A. Newcombe (eds.). "The Journal of Don Jacinto Caamaño," translated by Harold Grenfell, *British Columbia Historical Quarterly*, II (July-October, 1938), 189–222, 265–301.

Willoughby, Charles C. "Hats from the Nootka Sound Region," *American Naturalist*, XXXVII (1903), 65–68.

Wilson, Iris H. "Antonio Pineda y su viaje mundial," *Revista de Historia Militar*, VIII (1964), 49–64.

————. "Pineda's Report on the Beverages of New Spain," *Arizona and the West*, V (Spring, 1963), 79–90.

————. "Scientists in New Spain: The Eighteenth Century Expeditions," *Journal of the West*, I (July, 1962), 24–44.

————. "Spanish Scientists in the Pacific Northwest, 1790–1792," in *Reflections of Western Historians*, edited by John Alexander Carroll. Tucson: University of Arizona Press, 1960.

# INDEX

Abalone shell: used as container, 19; in fur trade, 95

Acapulco, 95

*Activo*: stocks used for Indians, 55; cost of, 96

Adultery: punishment for, 43

Agriculture: possibilities at Nootka, 7–8, 85; Alberni's efforts, 77–78

Agustín (servant of Maquinna): accused of crime, 55, 57

Alava, José de: Spanish commissioner at Nootka in 1795, 90n

Alberni, Capt. Pedro de: in command at Nootka, xxxviii; attempts at cultivation, 7; commands Catalonian Volunteers at Nootka, 77–80; regains friendship of Maquinna, 78; harmony with Nootka Indians, 79–80

Alcalá Galiano, Dionisio (commander of *Sutil*): expedition to Nootka, xiii, xl–xli; comments on "Noticias," xxvii; harmony with Nootka Indians, 80

Alcudia, Duke of: agreement on Nootka, li

Amat, Manuel de (Viceroy of Peru), 92n

Andía y Varela, José de: expedition to Tahiti, 92n

Animals, 6, 6n; catalogue of, 111–12

Apenas. *See* Izto-coti-clemot, Princess

*Aránzazu*: commanded by Jacinto Caamaño, xxiiin, xlivn

Archipelago de Carrasco, 93, 96

Archipelago of San Lázaro, 96

*Argonaut*: seizure of, xxxii, 74

Arrecifes: name bestowed by Cook, 65–66

Arteaga, Ignacio: expedition to Pacific Northwest, xliii

*Atrevida*: in Malaspina expedition, xxxviii

Baja California: venereal disease in, 43–44

Baker, Capt. James (of *Jenny*): skirmish with Wickinanish, 16, 71; names Sidman, 91n

Baranof, Alexander, viii

Barkley, Capt. Charles William (commander of *Imperial Eagle*), 69

Barkley Sound. *See* Archipelago de Carrasco

Barros Andrade, Juan de: witness, 69

Beverages: introduced by Spaniards, 21

Birds: at Nootka, 6, 6n; catalogue of, 112–13

Bodega y Quadra, Juan Francisco de la: Expedition of the Limits to the North of California ("Viaje de 1792"), xi, xxiii, xliv; 1792 journal of, xiii, xxiiin; gives instructions for northwest explorations, xxxvii–xxxviii; commissioned to settle Nootka Sound Controversy, xlii–xliii, l–li, 87–89; biographical sketch, xliii–xliv, xliiin; defends Indians, 55; friendship with Maquinna, 57; hears Maquinna's declaration, 69; documents of Nootka Sound Controversy, 73; to chart Northwest Coast with English, 83; harmony with Vancouver, 89

Boit, John: log of, xxxiii

Bonaechea, Capt. Domingo: commands expedition to Tahiti, 92n

Bonaparte, Joseph, lii

Boston-men: at Nootka, xxxiii–xxxiv, 74

Boxes, 18–19, 39

Broughton, William Robert: in Mexico, xlviii; on fur trade, 88

Brown, Capt. William (of *Butterworth*): skirmish with Wickinanish, 16, 71

Bucareli Inlet, xxxviii, 64, 93

Burial rites, 28–29

Bustamante y Guerra, José (commander of *Atrevida*), xxxviii, 80

Caamaño, Jacinto: expedition to Pacific Northwest, xlivn

Calendar: Nootkan method of dating, 61–63

California: Spain's future in, 1, 94–95; security of, 91; inhabitants of, 94; described, 94–95; in fur trade, 96–97

Cannibalism, 22–23

Canoes, 44–45, 47–48

Capes, 13–15, 49–50

Cardero, Josef: scribe of Alcalá Galiano-Valdés expedition, xiii

Carlos III of Spain, xxiv–xxvi, xxxiv

Carlos IV of Spain, xxvi, li–lii

Carmel, Mission of, 94

Carrasco, Bay of, xxxviii. *See also* Archipelago de Carrasco

Carreño, Alberto: editor of "Noti-

cias," xi–xiv; describes Moziño, xii

Catalonian Volunteers: under Alberni at Nootka, 77–80

Cedar: as hair decoration, 12; in construction of houses, 17n

*Chatham* (commanded by Broughton): departs for North America, 82

China: in fur trade, 97

Chinese: artisans at Nootka, xxxi; buyers of furs, 95; earnings of, 96

Cholula: textiles in, 95

Chronology, Nootkan, 61 ff.

Cla-sia-ca: stepmother of Izto-coti-clemot, 37

Clayoquot: in fur trade, 91, 96; mentioned, xxxviii, 76, 93

Clerke, Capt. Charles, 68

Colnett, Capt. James (commander of *Argonaut*): involvement in Nootka Sound Controversy, xxxii–xxxiii, 74–75; arrested by Martínez, 74–75; failure to sell otter skins, 88

*Columbia Rediviva* (commanded by John Kendrick): at Nootka, xxxiii, 70

Columbia River, 91

Commoners. *See Meschimes*

Cook, Capt. James: expedition to Nootka, xxix–xxx, 65–67; comments on Nootka, 3; on nose rings, 11; on use of iron and copper, 64; begins fur trade, 65; searches for Northwest Passage, 66–67; mentioned, viii

Cook Inlet, 82, 96

Copper: occurrence of, 5; value of, 42; use of, 50, 64; in Michoacán, 95; exported from New Spain, 97

Copti Mountains: site of puberty rites, 34; movement to, 41

Costanzó, Miguel: Moziño's professor, xlvi

Creation of man (Nootka legend), 26–27

# Index

Puberty rites: of Izto-coti-clemot, 34–37, 56

Quadra. *See* Bodega y Quadra, Juan Francisco de la
Qua-utz (God-Creator): confused with Spanish ship, xxviii, 66; described, 26; in puberty rites, 37; and creation of man, 61; mentioned, xlix
Quadra and Vancouver Island. *See* Vancouver Island
Quatlazape (brother of Maquinna): explains mourning ceremony, 29; participates in puberty rites, 35; religious sacrifice of, 39–40; power of, 57
Queen Charlotte Island: fur collection on, 91; potential fortification of, 93; mentioned, xxviii, 64
Quelequem (relative of Maquinna): sympathizes with English, 75; death of, 75–76, 78, 83
Querétaro: textiles in, 95
Quimper, Manuel (commander of *Princesa Real*), xxxvi–xxxvii
Quio-comasia: *tais* of Moachat confederacy, 31–32; name, 34; friendship with Spaniards, 56–57, 84; good health of father, 63; learns Spanish, 85

"Relación de la Isla de Mazarredo" (Yale MS), xii–xiii. *See also* "Noticias de Nutka"
Religion: plans for Spanish mission at Nootka, xxxiv, 85; of Nootka Indians, 25–30, 38–40
*Resolution*: in Cook's expedition, xxix, 67–68
Revilla Gigedo, Conde de (Viceroy of New Spain): biographical note, xxxvn; scientific projects in New Spain, xxxv–xli; instructs Bodega y Quadra on Nootka Sound Controversy, xlii; appoints Moziño, Maldonado, and Echeverría to ac-

company Bodega y Quadra, xliv, 83
Revilla Gigedo MS, xii. *See also* "Noticias de Nutka"
Rivera y Melo Montaño, Doña María Rita: wife of Moziño, xlv
Royal Academy of San Carlos: attended by Moziño, xlv; artists at, xlviii
Royal Botanical Garden of Mexico City, xxxv, xlvi
Royal and Pontifical University of Mexico, xlv
Royal Scientific Expedition to New Spain, xxxv, xlvi, li

Sahagún, Fray Bernardino de, ix
St. Helens, Baron of (Alleyne Fitzherbert): signs agreement on Nootka, li, 82
San Andrés de Tuxtla: volcano of, xi, xlvii
San Blas: investment in, 95
*San Carlos*: commanded by Fidalgo, xxxvi–xxxvii; commanded by Martínez at Nootka, 72
San Diego: port and garrison at, 94–95
Sandwich Islands (Hawaiian Islands): potential Spanish post, 92
San Estevan: named bestowed by Pérez, 65
San Francisco, Port of, 83, 94
San Lorenzo de Nutka: name given to Nootka by Pérez, xxviii, 66
San Rafael, Bay of, xxxviii
Santa Barbara Channel: port and garrison at, 94–95
*Santa Gertrudis*: cost of, 93
*Santiago*: commanded by Pérez, xxviii
Scientific activities: in eighteenth century, xxv, xxxiv–xxxvi
Sea otter: skins used in making garments, 14; methods of capture, 48; traded to Cook, 65; price of skins, 88, 97; in California, 94;

# Index

collection of, 96. *See also* Fur trade

Sessé, Martín (Director of Royal Scientific Expedition to New Spain): refers to Nootka manuscript, xii; praises Moziño, xxvii; work of expedition, xxxv–xxxvi; employs Moziño, xlvi; returns to Madrid, li

Shipping industry: in New Spain, 97

Sidman, Port of, 91

Sociedad Mexicana de Geografía y Estadística: publisher of *Noticias de Nutka*, xi–xii

Songs, 63

*Sonora*: commanded by Bodega y Quadra in 1775, xliii

Spaniards: friendship with Nootka Indians, 78, 83–84; poor conduct of sailors, 79, 84; potential as fur traders, 95–97

Spain: first contact with Nootka in 1774, xxviii–xxix, 65–66; claims to Pacific Northwest, xxxi, xli; occupation of Nootka in 1789, xxxi, 72–74; motives for settlement of Nootka, xxxiv; failure to establish mission, xxxiv, 85; future at Nootka and California, xlix–l, 90–93; settlement at Nootka, 7, 7n; security of possessions in New Spain and California, 91; problems of fortification, 93

Strait of Ferrer Maldonado (Northwest Passage): search for, xxxvii

Strait of Font, xxxviii

Strait of Heceta, xxxviii

Strait of Juan de Fuca: explorations of Quimper and Eliza, xxxvii–xxxviii, 77n, of Alcalá Galiano-Valdés, xl–xli, of Vancouver, xl–xli, 82; settlement proposed by Revilla Gigedo, xlii; entered by Vancouver, 87; fur collections at, 91, 96

*Sutil* (commanded by Valdés): at Nootka, xli

Tahiti: Spanish occupation of, 92

*Tais* (Nootka chief): functions of, 24–25; afterlife of, 28; veneration of, 29–30; hereditary rights of, 31–32; sacrifices of, 38–40; deeds of, 63; ages of, 63

*Taiscatlati* (brothers of the chief): functions of, 25; as second order of nobility, 32; friendship with Spaniards, 84

Tasis: winter quarters of Nootka Indians, 41

Tata-no: learns Spanish, 85

Temascaltepec: birthplace of Moziño, xliv–xlv

*Tlama*: sculptured figures, 18

Tlaumases: war against, 31, 63

Tlu-pana-nutl: *tais* of Moachat confederacy, 31–32; good health of father, 63; seizure of lumber in his village, 79; gifts to Alberni, 80

Tools, 50

Trade: of Nootka Indians, 64–65, 66. *See also* Fur trade

Trinidad, xxxviii

Tutusi, Chief, 29n, 65n

Tutusi, Island of (Cape Flattery), 65, 91

United States: relations with Spanish, xxxiii–xxxiv, 73; relations with Nootka Indians, 70–71. *See also* Boston-men

Valdés, Antonio: Spanish minister of Marine, xxxviii

Valdés, Cayetano (commander of *Sutil*): expedition to Nootka in 1792, xl–xli, 80

Vancouver, Capt. George (commander of *Discovery* and *Chatham*): commissioned to carry out Nootka settlement, xl–xli, 82; expedition to Nootka, xl–xli, 87; meeting with Alcalá Galiano and Valdés, xl–xli; on Nootka trade, 64–65; harmony with Nootka Indians, 80, 89; explores Strait of

PACIFIC OCEAN

Punta de Menzies

Islas de Berresford
(Scott Islands)

Archipielago de Broughton

Islas de Galiano y Valdés
(Nigei Island & Hope Island)

Cabo
Scot

ISLA DE QUADRA Y VANCOUVER

Estrecho de Johnstone

Puerto
de Brucks

Cabo Frondoso
(Cape Cook)

Bahía de la Esperanza

Isla de
Mazarredo

Puerto
de Nutca

Isla de Flores

Puerto de
Clayoquat
(Clayoquot Sound)   Isla
de Teran
(Vargas Island)